Total Community Library Service

Report
of a Conference
Sponsored by the
Joint Committee
of the
American Library
Association
and the
National Education
Association

Edited by
GUY GARRISON

AMERICAN
LIBRARY
ASSOCIATION
Chicago 1973

The Conference on Total Community Library Service
was made possible by a grant from the J. Morris Jones-
World Book Encyclopedia-ALA Goals Award Program
for 1971.

Library of Congress Cataloging in Publication Data

Conference on Total Community Library Service,
   Washington, D.C., 1972.
   Total community library service.

   Bibliography: p:
   1. Libraries and community—Congresses. I. Garrison,
Guy Grady, 1927-   ed. II. Joint Committee of the
American Library Association and the National Education
Association. III. Title.
Z716.4.C65 1972   025.5   73-4310
ISBN 0-8389-0149-2

Contents

Foreword

For as long as public schools and public libraries have existed in this country, they have worked together in various ways in the interest of education. As both schools and libraries have grown and changed to meet the needs of changing times, standards for library service have been established, and great strides have been made toward achieving the degree of excellence set forth in these standards for the various types of libraries to which they apply.

However, change is taking place in education, in community planning, in interlibrary cooperation, and in the technology for handling information through educational television, cable television, video cassettes, and reprography. These changes are leading many people—professional and layman alike—to question the separate institutional approach to library services as traditionally found in most communities. These questions about the overlapping roles and responsibilities of public libraries, school libraries, academic libraries, special libraries, and other educational resource agencies are being raised by administrators, fiscal personnel, legislators, educators, and librarians. Although the questions have frequently centered on one single point—the need for maintaining separate school and public libraries—the issue is, of course, much broader. However, vested interests of both school and public librarians and bad past experiences with inadequate services from both types of libraries, and from ill-conceived combinations of the two, have stood in the way of any widespread objective consideration of the total community approach to library service.

For many years, in fact since 1931, there has been a Joint Committee of the American Library Association and the National Education Association charged with the responsibility of exploring problems of mutual interest in the fields of library service and education, and with making recommendations to appropriate committees in the two associations. In its annual meetings, this Joint Committee has often taken up the question of shared responsibilities between public and school libraries. A policy statement, "The Public School and The Public Library: Partners in Community Development," was prepared for the October, 1967, meeting, was tabled at that time, but surfaced again in 1968 and 1969. During the meeting of October, 1969, the Joint Committee decided to appoint a subcommittee to come up with a working paper. At the October, 1970, meeting the subcommittee reported on its exploration of the problem, asked for an enlarged committee and a broader charge, and received the charge in the form of a hypothesis: "That coordination through joint planning of all existing information and library resources in a community will result in better services to meet all community information needs." Vague as it was, the hypothesis was a spur to action and the subcommittee developed a proposal.

This proposal took the form of a request to hold a conference and follow-up activities on the concept of total community library service. The proposal was submitted to the J. Morris Jones-World Book Encyclopedia-ALA Goals Award Program and asked for money to bring together for a three day conference a group representing school, public, and academic libraries; community planners and sociologists; teachers; governmental officials; and school administrators to explore the problem.

This proposal was successful in competition with many other worthy projects submitted for consideration in early 1971. The award was made to the ALA-NEA Joint Committee to bring together in Washington, D.C., on May 11-13, 1972, a small group of persons who could attempt to define the concept of total community library service and to suggest ways in which all the libraries of a community working together might achieve this goal.

The publication of the proceedings from the conference is part of the follow-up activities designed by the Joint Committee to see that the impetus generated by the meeting in Washington is not lost, and that the dialogue between librarians, educators, and others interested in library services and educational resources is continued.

There was unanimous agreement among conference participants that planning for library services, now and in the future, must involve all of the interested agencies, and that coordination of activities, services, resources, and even facilities is not only feasible but desirable depending on the needs of the community to be served.

The discussions and the recommendations clearly point to the need for strong professional leadership in developing interagency planning at the local community level. The setting of educational objectives and the development of scientific methods for measuring attainment of these objectives are imperative before basic changes in the structure of library service are undertaken. The need was clearly expressed for a sharing of information about present and proposed research and demonstration projects concerned with a multiagency approach to library service. Some cautions were expressed that the rationale for change from the status quo be carefully developed and not based on expediency or on supposed weaknesses in one or another of the institutions now involved in the delivery of library services.

The conference did not develop a certain blueprint for the achievement of total community library service. It did open up for serious discussion a topic which will have great implications for the future of library service. By means of this publication and through other planned follow-up activities in the NEA and the ALA, the Joint Committee hopes to share the excitement of the conference and to stimulate further demonstration efforts aimed at multiagency coordination in the delivery of library service.

GRACE SLOCUM
Conference Chairman

Preface

This book grows out of the Conference on Total Community Library Service held in Washington, D.C., on May 11-13, 1972, under the sponsorship of the Joint Committee of the American Library Association and the National Education Association. It brings to a wider audience the papers, critiques, summaries of discussion, and recommendations that were part of the conference, as well as some supplementary material which relates closely to the topic under discussion.

The papers by A. Harry Passow, Edmond R. Coletta, Gerald R. Brong, and Kathleen Molz were prepared as background information and were available as preprints to all conferees. In their published form here, they are basically unchanged from the preprints. These papers were summarized briefly by their authors at the conference, were critiqued respectively by J. Lloyd Trump, Roderick G. Swartz, Robert Heinich, and Mildred Frary, and served as a basis for small group discussions involving all participants. The critiques were given informally and were later transcribed and edited from tapes, as were the summaries of the small group discussions.

An important part of the book consists of the recommendations for action that came out of the small group discussions. A word about the development of the recommendations may be helpful. Each discussion group had a discussion leader and each group was required to turn in notes after each session in the form of recommendations. These notes, along with the summaries made by representatives from each discussion group, were the basis for the list of recommendations. The list, along with copies of the edited papers, were presented to the full Joint Committee at its October, 1972, meeting, and the recommendations were scrutinized, amplified, and tightened. In its present form the list of recommendations represents what the Joint Committee sees as the major recommendations stemming from the conference.

The material added to this publication which was not part of the conference consists of a bibliographical essay and two profiles of demonstration projects involving multiagency library service.

It was apparent from the beginning that some form of bibliography or bibliographic essay would be needed since the conference topic, Total Community Library Service, is a vague one, and since the literature on the subject is widely scattered. An annotated bibliography was prepared for the use of the conference planning committee by Dennis McDonald, a student at the University of Maryland School of Library and Information Services. In the process of preparing the papers from the conference for publication, the editor had the assistance of Joyce Post, a bibliographical assistant at the Drexel University Graduate School of Library Science, to do further work on material relating to the backgrounds of community library service. Her resulting bibliographic essay seemed to be so helpful in clarifying the concept that the decision was made by the Joint Committee to include it in this publication as an appendix.

During the conference itself, two research and demonstration projects currently underway with USOE support were mentioned time and time again as good examples of the multiagency approach to library service. These were the project in Olney, Texas, that is seeking to merge the school and public library services, and the Action Library in Philadelphia, a demonstration library jointly supported by the Philadelphia School District, the Free Library of Philadelphia, the Archdiocesan Schools of Philadelphia, and some of the independent private schools of Philadelphia. The profile of the Olney project was prepared by James Kitchens, the project director, for inclusion in this publication. The profile of the Action Library by Lowell A. Martin, the project consultant, is reprinted here with his permission.

GUY GARRISON
Proceedings Editor

Trends in Learning and Education Affecting Community Library Services

Presentation:
A. HARRY PASSOW

Response:
J. LLOYD TRUMP

In surveying trends in learning and education that might have a bearing on community library services, several problems are immediately apparent. For one thing, in a field which seems especially prone to faddism, there is always difficulty in distinguishing between a *trend* and a *fad*. For instance, the "open classroom" is currently receiving a good deal of attention, with both the lay press and professional journals fanning interest in the notion. Are we experiencing a trend—a general direction—toward the widespread adoption of the concept of an open classroom, or is this yet another bandwagon onto which educators are jumping? Another problem is the fact that *all* elements of the educational process—content, methods, personnel, resources, organization, climate, etc.—could indeed have a bearing on community library services, depending on how such services are conceived. Quite obviously, the stereotype of the community library as a warehouse for books, periodicals, and newspapers has long been outmoded. It is not just that community libraries have or are becoming "media centers," but that they are now providing a variety of other services and resources which are essentially educative in nature. Still another problem is that of delineating the "trend"—how global or specific should the aspect of education be? Should one consider "Sesame Street," or the phenomenon of television technology, as

A. Harry Passow is Jacob H. Schiff Professor of Education at Teachers College, Columbia University.

J. Lloyd Trump is Associate Secretary for Research and Development, National Association of Secondary School Principals, Washington, D.C.

a trend? A good many other problems could be stated, but the above should suffice to indicate that the items chosen for discussion here are significant trends as perceived by one educator, and that for the term *trends*, words like developments, innovations, or promising approaches might be substituted.

There has been a recognition that many agencies, institutions, and settings other than the institution called "school" educate. The family, home, neighborhood, and peer culture all provide educative settings and all affect learning. Such learning consists of knowledge, skills, values, attitudes, motivations, and self-concepts, some of which are consonant and valued by schools, but many of which may actually conflict with the more formal goals of the school. Both the Coleman Report *(Equality of Educational Opportunity)* [1] and the Plowden Report *(Children and Their Primary Schools)* [2] raise questions about the relative influence that the school brings to bear on a child's achievement, compared with that of his background and the general social context. Clearly, both are inextricably bound. Environmental and experiential factors exert a strong influence on the child's attainment during early, as well as later, years and on affective, as well as cognitive, growth. In preadolescence and adolescence, the peer culture is an especially strong influence on what is learned. These influences affect both the substance, as well as the processes, of learning. This idea, that the family, community, and various institutions educate and influence learning is, of course, not new. What is new is that educators have become more sensitive to these multiple influences on learning, and so are taking them into account in structuring teaching and learning opportunities.

The thrust, for example, for what is known as "early intervention" is based on the belief that the educating resources available to poor families are limited and the values different from those of the school, so that the school must "intervene" to insure that the needs and services required for success in the classroom are provided. However, it is obvious that the poor child, like other children, is learning, in that he is acquiring knowledge, insights, values, motives, and skills which shape his behavior and form the basis for his performance in the classroom. The notion of "experiential deprivation"—the absence of books and magazines in the home, the paucity of educative toys, the unavailability of intellectual stimulation—has undergone considerable reappraisal in recent years. Even in the poorest environment, the child learns significant coping and survival skills, and educators are turning their attention to these as a basis on which to build more formal and structured learning opportunities. Learning theories today are being modified to take into account differences in learning styles, interaction of forces in the environment which affect learning, and various means by which individuals process, interpret and internalize information.

There is a trend toward the development of more relevant curriculum and instruction. Responding to the argument that much of what is taught in today's schools is irrelevant for the student, there are efforts being made to provide more meaningful and appropriate instruction. Criticisms of existing programs as obsolete and irrelevant take a variety of forms, including the withdrawal of students seeking alternative experiences.

A decade ago, curriculum efforts tended to be concentrated on improving instruction through the subject disciplines. Committees and commissions attempted to provide students with an operational understanding of the structure of the subject discipline, engaging students in inquiry modes by which they might better understand the methods of the discipline. The consequence of these efforts was the development of the so-called new math, new physics, new social studies (anthropology, geography, and history as separate disciplines), and other subjects. Often, the program involved the production of educational packages consisting of text and nontext materials, supplementary multimedia materials, and resources for teachers. These packages vary in the flexibility provided in subject discipline coverage, in the alternative media available, and the extent to which inquiry and creativity are encouraged and stimulated. They vary in the extent to which they are sequential and cumulative, and the degree with which they are organized about meaningful concepts and knowledge units.

Interest in the discipline-centered curricula continues, but there is an upsurge in concern for problem-centered curricula, which are interdisciplinary in nature. For example, Krug notes that

> some leading spokesman in social studies [suggest] that the newest social studies revolution will move in the direction of an interdisciplinary social studies curriculum which would obliterate the boundaries between history, sociology, and anthropology and draw on concepts, research, and methods from all of the social sciences. Furthermore, the new social studies curricula would center more on the affective domain, the realm of values and attitudes, and would evolve around the individual and his interaction with society, war and peace, ecology, and the interests of students. [3]

Such curricula efforts would use subject disciplines differently, would deal more directly with social realities and concerns, would deal with values and value conflicts as these are found in the student's world. Youth are no longer content with the antiseptic programs which avoid the real problems and issues which they all confront and which may feel they must tackle if their education is to have relevance. The intrinsic and legitimate connection between social reality and the school program and between the development of insights into the processes and problems of society and the individual are being viewed as pertinent foci for curriculum development efforts. Such a trend naturally leads to different relationships between student and teacher, school and society. Relevant curricula deal not only with knowledge acquisition, but with affective behaviors as well.

There is a trend toward humanizing the school as an institution, and toward developing a more humane education. A number of critics, writing from differing stances, have attacked the school as a dehumanized, impersonal, repressive institution in which human ends have become subservient to bureaucratic means. Some describe the school as a "knowledge factory" in which new hardware provides efficient ways to dispense more information, but which leaves students alienated, frustrated, and uninvolved. Calling the school "a heritage of inhumaneness," Foshay observes:

> Instead of treating students as individual human beings, we group, track, segregate, stereotype. It is not surprising that the students, learning the hidden lesson in such practices, do the same thing to one another and to their elders. Instead of treating education as an opportunity for a child to grow into a man, we treat it as a race for grades and reflect the societal demand for competition. It is not surprising that the more thoughtful students ultimately reject the game [4]

One trend has been the move toward restructuring and redesigning the school, with proposals ranging from "deschooling society" to so-called "free schools," alternative schools, or schools-within-a-school; from loosening schedules and modifying the factory image of the school to flexible, self-structured, highly individualized programs; from a facilitating participation in planning and governance to creating a different reward system for students and teachers.

There has been a trend toward concern with affective education—what Sterling McMurrin refers to as "the emotions, the passions, the dispositions, the motives, the moral and esthetic sensibilities, the capacity for feeling, concern, attachment or detachment, sympathy, empathy, and appreciation." [5] The affective domain is beginning to receive attention as a relevant content of instruction, a component of motivation for learning, and as a means of encouraging personal development. The concern with so-called sensitivity training/education is one trend toward an understanding of self and one's impact on others. Such education, as Wells points out, "legitimizes the current feelings, values, attitudes, and concerns of learners and helps them develop methods for successfully managing these life forces as they move toward full humanness." [6]

The dissatisfaction with school and schooling is, in many ways, a reflection of the contradictions and dissonances in the larger society —poverty amidst affluence, concern for others coupled with consummate selfishness, racism, powerlessness, isolation and impersonalization even within crowds. The young are keenly aware of the manifestations of these conditions and have forced schools to modify those aspects of education with which they will deal. They are forcing schools to remove the rigidities, the institutional restraints, and the personal hang-ups of educators that block nurturing humaneness.

There is a trend toward moving teaching and learning out into the community. The idea of a community school is not a new one; the concept was used back in the 1930s, particularly in small towns and rural areas, to denote the school as the educational hub for children and adults. That concept has both broadened and been altered. In some instances, the school has become a center for community services and activities, in addition to serving as an educating agency. In other instances, the community is conceived as a total education environment, within which the institution called school is but one component. Thus, the relationships between the school and the community (or communities) of which it is a part can vary, and labels such as "community school," "community-centered school," or "school-centered community" reflect different kinds of transactions and constraints, different uses of resources.

Recently, there has been a development of the concept of the community as classroom, exemplified in part by the "school without walls," in which the school literally is the community, and the students are educated in and by the community. The use of the community as an educative resource can range from an occasional field trip or community-based inquiry or project to the widely publicized Parkway School in Philadelphia, which uses various institutions and agencies in the community as vehicles for education. The Parkway Program has been called "a school without its *own* walls."

Further, there is the concept of the community as teacher—that is, the problems and resources of the community provide the instructional context. Aside from its cultural resources, the community can provide for work experience and service which are effective learning opportunities.

If this trend toward a reconception of the relationships between school and community continues, it will mean different kinds of programs, personnel utilization, space arrangements, and organization in the school. If the total community becomes the educational setting, then the community library, as one of the components of that setting, will have to reformulate its roles and services. Since communities differ in their needs and capabilities, varied services will be required, depending in part on the educative resources available through other institutions and agencies, including the school.

There has been a trend toward the development of a variety of learning and teaching resources, the application of technology to instruction, and the building of instructional systems. This trend is apparent in the variety of instructional media now available—print and nonprint, visual and audio, electronic and mechanical, symbolic and illustrative, real and simulated, learner- and teacher-controlled. It is also apparent in the development of multimedia centers, learning systems, and what is called "total instructional environments." Perhaps the most significant change has been the shift of focus from audiovisual aids designed essentially to be used by the teacher, to multimediated resources which the learner controls, which provide a variety of materials and strategies appropriate for attaining his objectives. The multimediated learning environment makes available information sources, processes, and learning strategies not otherwise available, and creates new roles for the teacher.

Now available to learner and teacher are a variety of resources, some of which are simply minor improvements on traditional materials, such as the filmstrip projector and record player. Others are complex and comprehensive instructional systems—computer-based and computer-assisted instruction, television and videotaping equipment, programmed instruction, dial access and retrieval systems. Such media vary in many ways: whether or not literacy is required for use, the sense modalities involved, the user flexibility, degree of user control, content (e.g., information processing or storing, testing, simulation), extent of individualization, individual or group use intended.

The more traditional resources, such as books, blackboards, and projectors, continue to be used, of course, with a considerable increase in the student and/or teacher involvement in the production of films, tapes, and other display and informational materials. Such productions may be for the purpose of developing resources to be used by other students or classes for instructional purposes, or they may aim at developing communication or persuasion skills for those involved in the activities. Increasingly, there is an interest in developing a variety of kinds of literacy in addition to print literacy.

Multimediated learning centers permit teachers to play very different roles in the classrooms. For example, using tapes, cassettes, 8mm film, and other materials, the teacher can organize instruction so that it is highly individualized, with pupils working by themselves or in groups while the teacher becomes an arranger of learning engagements, a facilitator of learning, and a manager of instructional resources. Media can provide greater freedom and flexibility for both student and teacher, and pupils can use such resources in school and out. For example, with increased availability of cassette tape recorders, students can take cassette tapes home or prepare them at home, extending access to master teachers or experiences of many kinds.

The use of a variety of individualized materials makes it possible for students to work at their own pace and to engage in learning experiences which are highly personal. While the promise of programmed instruction has not been fully realized as yet, the potential for individualization still exists and may yet come with greater sophistication of both hardware and software. Traditional resources such as books represent considerable flexibility and individualization, depending on how they are used. Tape recorders, 8mm projectors, science lab kits, and many other media permit access to information not otherwise readily available to the student and the teacher.

Another development has been the increase in the use of simulations and games in teaching and learning. Simulations may involve complex computerized programs in which the student is presented with information about a particular situation, is called on to solve problems, and is able to observe the consequences of his decision. Other simulations may involve several media, including print, films, filmstrips, and tapes. The use of games for instructional purpose (in contrast to recreational ends) has a sound psychological and learning theory base, with certain skills and insights being acquired by employing a strategy which is both challenging, interesting, and entertaining.

New media are also being used in teacher education and as a means of improving instruction. Videotapes provide a means for teachers to analyze their own classroom behavior using microteaching techniques, wherein a sequence is taped, critiqued, and retaught. Videotapes are also used for teacher training involving presentation of information, observation of master teachers, and skill development through simulations.

As the concept of multimedia instructional resources has expanded, school libraries have also changed in terms of the services and resources available and the organization and facilities for the delivery of these services. School media programs have become centered in the library. The converted closet, in which audiovisual materials were stored to be checked out by teachers, is being padlocked, and the library or a satellite center has become the locus of resources for learning and teaching. Mediated instructional resources have become crucial to present educational strategies.

There is a trend toward education for cultural pluralism. The events of the past two decades—the civil rights movement, the war on poverty, the deterioration of the cities, the continuing value and identity crises of American society—have exposed serious flaws in the ideals and idealism which schools have presumably attempted to perpetuate. The myth of the melting pot has been examined and racism—individual and institutional—has been laid bare. As Abrahams put it, "The melting pot ideology then has always been an essentially nationalistic one, and thus an argument subject to uses by any group, which preaches Americanism at the expense of ethnic, regional, or even social class identification." [7]

There have been efforts to develop programs which build on group and individual cultural identity and nurture cultural pluralism at the same time. The concern with developing racial and ethnic identity has resulted in reassessment of content in existing courses, in the developing of new courses, and in the reappraisal and development of instructional materials and resources. Minority groups, racial and ethnic, have taken seriously the notion of building a power base and cultural identification as a means of attaining equality. Blacks, Chicanos, Puerto Ricans, and American Indians have moved toward separatism, local control, and a recognized identity which appears to be counter to moves for integration. Yet the Urban Education Task Force suggests that these thrusts are not antithetical to the aims of integration, but rather that

> This emergent—and newest—thrust seems to hold potentially the greatest promise to achieving genuine integration since it concomitantly recognizes common goals (e.g., economic self-sufficiency, a healthful environment, improved educational programs) and proposes to work cooperatively on the ways to achieve them. [8]

The growth in racial and ethnic studies in schools has raised a variety of questions: What are appropriate goals for such programs? What should the content consist of? Who should participate? Who should teach such courses? Should such studies be separate from or integrated into the regular educational program? Underlying this trend is a basic issue: will this development reduce racism and ethnic hostility and build a stronger, more viable society?

There has been a trend toward the development of early childhood programs, from infancy to primary school. Such programs take a variety of forms—nursery schools, day care centers, preschool programs, etc. The focus of such programs varies considerably. Some are based on evidence that the first five or six years of life are particularly critical in the cognitive and affective development of the child. Others are grounded in the notion that conceptual learning sets, interests, and attitudes are better established during the early years and provide the basis for more effective later learning. Still others stem from the idea of "experiential deprivation"—that with poverty, child-rearing practices and home environment can result in limited language and cognitive development, as well as socializing experiences different from those of the middleclass—which must be compensated for in an educational setting. Some programs have more simple goals: to care for children while mothers are working.

Just as such programs vary with respect to the basis for organization, they differ in the program goals and objectives, the structure of the curriculum and instructional procedures, the resources available, the nature of staff and adult roles, the involvement of parents, and the use of space and time. Project Head Start involved hundreds of thousands of preschoolers in thousands of programs across the land, programs which differed widely in their conceptual and operational frameworks, as well as their qualitative outcomes. "Sesame Street," an educational television program, reaches a wide audience of preschool children with programming intended to develop preacademic skills and positive attitudes toward learning. Other projects were much more modest in scope and aim.

Early childhood programs have varied in the nature and extent of parent involvement. "Sesame Street," for instance, produced a series of parent guides which were aimed at the education of parents. Other programs have aimed at restructuring maternal teaching patterns, for example, or at developing new child-rearing practices. Some have actually focused more on parent education and home and family life than on preschool learnings. As a consequence, parents have sought resources in the community through which they can participate in the development of their children along lines advocated by the designers of early childhood programs. The downward extension of educational opportunities seems to have been established as a firm trend which affects the school and its programs. It has made clearer the idea of parents as teachers, and the need for education for parenthood.

There has been a trend toward further (postcompulsory), continu-

ing, and recurring education. Opportunities for education beyond the
compulsory years of education—education for career development
or personal growth—have expanded considerably in the post-World
War II years. A good deal of expansion has taken place in the formal
systems of the two- and four-year colleges and universities and in
adult education programs. A good deal of growth has taken place
under different auspices, often less formal. For example, the use of
educational television for instructional purposes, such as "Sunrise
Semester," community-centered discussion and problem-solving
groups, and cultural development groups constitute further legitimate education opportunities. There has been a sharp increase in
the number of young people and adults involved in the College Level
Examination Program (credit by examination) and in credit for experience, whereby the individual's life experiences are assessed and
translated into college credits.

Continuing and recurring education implies the possibility of
either regular or intermittent educational experiences occurring during much of the individual's life, with more or less regular training
and retraining in connection with his work or opportunities for personal development not connected with a career. One component of
such programs is the so-called New Careers and Career Ladder Programs, aimed essentially at the undereducated and under-or unem-
ployed. The New Careers approach focuses on the human service
occupations (in schools, hospitals, community development and recreation areas), attempts to restructure some aspects of such services
so that individuals with minimal retraining can quickly be involved
in fulfilling necessary functions, and enables the individual to move
up on the career ladder by acquiring additional skills and knowledge.
Paraprofessionals and aides are the largest constituencies for such
programs for upgrading an individual's education. Because such
programs are often not under the auspices of the formal educational
system, participants and staffs must turn to the community for
necessary learning resources.

A specific case of continuing education is that of in-service education for teachers. Many of the traditional modes of in-service education (courses, workshops, etc.) continue, but new programs are
emerging. These involve such approaches as videotape microteaching
techniques, simulation packages, community studies, and computer-
based instruction.

*There has been a trend toward differentiated staffing and the in-
volvement of a variety of persons other than traditional professionals in teaching roles.* The differentiated staffing concept often carries
with it the idea of career ladders, involvement of teams in teaching,

and varied patterns of organization for instruction. Although there are many variations of differentiated staffing, the term often

> implies subdividing the global role of the teacher into different professional and paraprofessional subroles according to specific functions and duties that need to be performed in the schools and according to particular talents and strengths that are evident within the human resources of any given school community. Some differentiated staffing models also include the creation of a hierarchy, with job responsibilities that are commensurate with the range of pay. [9]

Another development has been one of involving individuals in the teaching process other than the traditional, certified professionals. The mushrooming of tutoring programs, both in and out of school, and the growth of school volunteer programs have demonstrated the contributions of such individuals to the development of youngsters who appear to profit from one-to-one, highly personalized relationships. High school and college students, for example, have proved effective as tutors for peers and younger children. Citizens from the community have served as rich resource personnel, filling a variety of educational needs. They have provided enriched experiences for students who capitalize on the expertise, specialization, and experience of nonprofessionals as teachers. The concept of "learning from one another"—students from students, students from adults and vice versa—has been demonstrated to be a sound one. Within classes, peer teaching and learning groups, have proved to be effective.

There is a trend toward alternative forms of schooling. As indicated earlier, dissatisfaction with many aspects of existing forms of schooling has led to a search for alternatives. For one thing, as Doll points out, education and school are often not perceived as synonymous terms: "[Youth] believe education literally fills their entire life space; yet they see schooling as properly occupying only a section of that space." [10] Altered conceptions of education and the educative function, coupled with other kinds of dissatisfactions, have resulted in the development of different forms of schooling. Some alternatives represent restructuring within the traditional school system—e.g., open education or informal classrooms, personalized secondary education programs, school-community learning laboratories, minischools, etc. Others are found considerably outside the traditional school setting—e.g., storefront schools, street academies, free schools and school communes, etc. These new forms of schooling rely rather heavily on the community for their educational resources. For instance, their library resources are often quite meager and they depend on community libraries to help meet the needs of students and staff. Instructional materials are frequently in short supply. The development of new schools and new forms of schooling affect the relationships with other educative institutions and agencies and the kinds of resources required.

Other trends might be cited, and those which have been listed could be interpreted differently. Nevertheless, what quite clearly appears is that education and learning are being conceived quite differently at the present time, and that the means, forms, and structures for educating must be reconceived as well. As one bright youngster put it:

> Instead, these men and women should think about the contributions to education made by television, paperbacks, radio, clubs, trade unions, businesses, Sunday schools, community programs, and the corners where kids hang out. School doesn't touch a lot of the real education we get. [11]

Several implications for total community library services emerge from the trends described above:

1. Community libraries are obviously something more than supplementary education centers; they are centers in which considerable teaching and learning takes place, of both a formal and informal nature. In planning the kinds of services the library is to provide, this educative function should be central, not incidental.

2. Consideration of the community library's education role might include attention to the library as an extension of the home and neighborhood. For example, during the critical early childhood years, the library can contribute to the cognitive and affective growth of children as well as to parental, home, and family education.

3. Community libraries must consider the full range of media available presently and how these can be used most effectively by their clientele. For instance, as knowledge and information storehouses, computers make possible retrieval far more effectively than other print media. How can the community library use computers, dial access, and other electronic media for storing and retrieving information for library users?

4. In becoming media centers, community libraries should extend the range of resources—print and nonprint, visual and audio, electronic and mechanical. In addition, libraries might provide toys and artifacts for borrowing, just as some presently make it possible to borrow works of art. For instance, there is no reason why 8mm cartridge films could not be available for borrowing just as tapes, records, and books can be borrowed presently. Multisensory media might be made easily available.

5. Community libraries should consider different ways of organizing space and developing the total environment. The *silence* signs have been taken down, comfortable reading corners have been created, viewing rooms and listening centers established, and other significant changes affected. Should community libraries provide the equivalent of the corner hangout or mothers' coffee klatch? Should the community library consider the impact of a total learning setting on library users?

6. Community libraries should consider ways of moving services out into the neighborhoods where they are readily accessible to potential users. Many libraries have gone far beyond the "branch," out into the storefront, shopping center, supermarket, and even the laundromat. The "drop-in" library need not be staffed in the traditional fashion. Moving into the community will enable libraries to reach a clientele which has not taken advantage of available services.

7. The trend toward cultural pluralism and the elimination of racism requires a reassessment of the library's role in terms of its services and resources. What contributions can the library make to nurturing cultural identity and building pride in self? What responsibilities does the library have toward the reduction of racism? How can library services contribute to cultural pluralism?

8. While considering new ways of providing for cognitive growth and the dissemination of knowledge, libraries need consider ways of contributing to the affective growth of their clientele—values, emotions, attitudes, etc. What kinds of services will involve the library in the real world and overcome any vestiges of its antiseptic image?

9. As young people and adults become more involved in continuing education and schooling outside the places called school and college, the community libraries will be asked to provide a variety of resources other than those traditionally supplied. What kinds of changes will have to be made in order to meet these needs?

10. As "Sesame Street," "The Electric Company," and other educational television programs tend toward more direct instruction, community libraries may have to provide for an early childhood population, complete with parents, who have been encouraged to become library users. What kinds of services and resources will be useful for this younger population and for the parents who accompany them?

11. As groups become more sensitive to community problems and their responsibilities for participation in problem-solving activities, the community libraries may be called on to provide a variety of resources which might be used in studying such problems and seeking solutions. Such a requirement could call for different information retrieval and delivery systems than those which have become more familiar.

12. If the concept of "learning from one another" is taken seriously,

the community library could contribute to facilitating the means by which various individuals could become involved in the education and development of others. The rich human resources of a community could be used by the community library, as well as the school and other agencies.

13. The press for community control, involvement in decision-making, and the exercise of power which is currently centering on the schools could soon encompass the community library as well. How can community libraries be made more responsive to the needs of the communities and populations they are supposed to serve, and how can they be made more accountable?

In conclusion, insofar as education is concerned, schools and community libraries are, or should be, partners in a joint venture. The community library does not exist simply to provide supplementary services. Both the community library and the schools are educative institutions and must strive constantly to find ways of working together for the benefit of the children, youth, and adults of our society. In the quest for providing equality of educational opportunity, libraries and schools have joint responsibilities.

Response | Mr. Trump

Dr. Passow has given us a relatively conventional paper about what is happening in education today. Unfortunately, these are not trends, so much as myths of change. They are not trends but wishful thinking by educators, based on a few outstanding examples. Also, an approach of this type which highlights trends ignores many of the community forces, and even some of the forces within education itself, that effectively block the kind of progress illustrated by these trends—progress that many people have been trying to institutionalize for decades.

His paper ably covers most of the current trends in learning and education, albeit without much emotional commitment. He is less successful at suggesting what bearing these trends might have on the concept of total community library service. He concludes that libraries basically should follow the example of what is going on in schools. We have community-based schools, so we should have community-based libraries; we have better audiovisual services in schools, so we should have better audiovisual services in libraries (I only hope the libraries will do it better). We are paying more attention to preschool children and to continuing education in schools; therefore the same should be true of libraries. Schools are involving the community in decision-making; so should libraries.

How about some fire? Some real issues? As schools and libraries get closer together in function as educational agencies, why are they still separate? If they are to be both alike, why do we waste time and money on separate schools and libraries? Separately trained personnel? Separate boards and taxing bodies? Where does one stop, and the other begin? Who owns 4:30 P.M.? Who owns Saturday? Sunday? Who owns July?

Actually, libraries are well advanced over schools in making use of modern concepts of education, since they take you where you are, let you teach yourself, and are open when you need them. The big thing in schools right now is the discovery that children can teach each other and themselves, and that they learn more out of the classroom than in the classroom. Libraries have known that for a long time. Only in our time are we beginning to undo the harm done to the schools a century or so ago when they brought in the graded system from Germany, and seventy years ago when the universities gave us the Carnegie Unit. If libraries were a little better at keeping records of what they do, they could tell educators a lot about how individuals pursue learning on their own. If community library service based on coordination of libraries and schools becomes more than a concept, what are we going to do to keep track of what people learn in libraries? How will the schools get along without the competititve marking system?

Dr. Passow deplores the overemphasis in schools on the subject disciplines. Maybe he should deplore the rigidity of the Dewey Decimal Classification as an approach to organizing materials. As we talk more about total community library service, we must decide what the essential elements are, and which part of the educational establishment—public school, public library, community college, etc.—could best supply them. Regardless of where the resource collection is located, we have to think of better ways to make it easy for people to get at what they want. Why not try arranging materials in ways that have some meaning to people? Librarians could help by experimenting with the division of materials by level, rather than by subject matter. A library that is really useful might be divided by level according to the following plan:

1. A basic educational collection level—things that are essential for everyone to know.
2. A hobby and amateur collection level where materials are available if you want to learn more about subjects.
3. A career specialist and research level where materials are located that are of interest only to specialists.

Regardless of where the learning resources are located, we have to face up to making a community library a stimulating, rewarding, individualized learning environment that motivates, provides options and alternatives, and recognizes how the home, the school, the total community (particularly the institutionalized aspects such as libraries, museums, and other facilities) complement each other. Certainly as we move into a broader approach to library service, we have to justify the money and the time spent on this service by teachers and librarians, and on developing the new institutional arrangements we need.

Since Dr. Passow's paper on trends in education did not get into the thorny problems of barriers to educational progress, I think it is very appropriate to warn people who are thinking about a new kind of service, a new kind of institution, a community library that is also educational, to recognize elements in our society that oppose change in schools—and, by extension, in all of our educational agencies. As you try to develop new ways of delivering library service, you are going to run into the same problems that have kept us, in the schools, from realizing these wonderful trends. These problems will let you go a little way, but will prevent you from doing what you want to do. I suspect that you will run into all of these barriers, and I am not just talking about money barriers, since they are the least important. Money is not a big problem; we can always get money one way or another, but these are the barriers that really count:

1. The university professors. They write text books, and see all students, even in the elementary and secondary schools, as potential students in their own classes and prospective professional people. They are the ones that keep us from liberalizing the curriculum. They are the ones who make us teach a lot of stuff to kids that they neither want nor need.

2. High school teachers. The second force that opposes us every place we go are the high school teachers. They are primarily committed to their subject fields, and don't think any child can survive without knowing certain things which are very close to their own hearts. In practice and belief they are close to the university professor.

3. Secondary school principals and their assistants. These are people who have developed security in their present practices and who enjoy the prestige of their present positions—the community limelight, the extracurricular activities, and the other side benefits of their jobs. They feel insecure with methods of teaching and learning, with curriculum, and the like. They don't know how to adapt to change or how to organize an environment for learning. I suspect that the same is true for a lot of library administrators.

4. The extreme rightists. A fourth barrier we contend with all the time in education is the extreme rightist element in our society. They regard any change in education as communist-inspired. They constantly use such terms as "child-centered," "progressive education," "permissive," and "undisciplined," as dirty words, without bothering to understand the meanings. These are the words that they use in every letter to the editor, in every open meeting, etc. They don't know what the terms mean, but they turn off a lot of people, and if a new community library concept is to take hold, it has to have a lot of novelty and change associated with it, and these changes will be opposed.

5. Teacher organizations. The teacher organizations, of course, are a major enemy to change because they are the ones who see a threat in anything we do that changes the present alignment of teaching. If you suggest, for instance, that someone can learn something from a person who is not appropriately credentialed, who hasn't had the required number of hours in education, then you are in trouble with the organizations. Organizations see change as a threat to the number of teachers, the salary schedule, the size of classes. The whole concept of differentiated staffing is about to go down the drain because of violent opposition from organized teachers. Organizations like to say that they are promoting education, but when the chips are down, they oppose change. They tend to believe that the only way to improve education is through smaller classes and higher salaries.

6. Conformist students. A barrier to change is also found in the conformist student who has succeeded well in the conventional school, and is afraid of such things as community decision-making, increased responsibility for individual learning, etc. We say that we need increased responsibility for students, but there are many conformist students who don't want freedom and responsibility, who want to prolong their dependency. These conformists, of course, are not all students. Many retain the characteristic into their 30s, 40s, and 50s.

7. The "3Rs" crowd. We always have problems with persons who oppose anything above the minimal school program. They are really against high schools, they deplore fancy buildings, they are against professionally trained teachers, they oppose educational specialists such as counselors and librarians, they see no use for anything beyond simple reading, writing, and arithmetic, plus maybe a little science and history. They ask only for a "good basic education." When you start doing all these fancy things about restructuring library service, these are the people who will say, "What's wrong with books?" "Why do you need all this fancy stuff?" "The good books are

all we need, forget about all these programs, all this remedial reading, all this adult education."

8. Conformist philosophers. There is a sizable group whose learning philosophy really emphasizes conformity and memorization as opposed to creativity, cultivation of higher mental processes, and the like. They think children are somewhat like rats; they ought to memorize a few things and react to certain stimuli, and that's about all. They think that the mind is a muscle, that it is trained in the same way as the muscles in the arm. They don't see any need for frivolity in education, they oppose group activities, they adore punishment and reward, they see no reason for individualized education.

All of these are real barriers to educational change, and they are barriers which you will have to consider if you really believe in the community library concept. Be prepared, and try to get a jump on the enemy. I have encountered all of these problems in education, and have learned it the hard way. This conventional wisdom should temper your eagerness to explore the kinds of trends in learning and education that Dr. Passow reported.

There is another question that needs to be explored. How are you going to motivate people to make use of total community library service? Some people will use it regardless of where it is or what it is. Others require motivation. We have a lot of very strange ways of motivating students in school, but in actual practice, most of what happens is self-motivation. Are you ready to accept accountability for the increased money we will spend, the increased professional staff we will need, and the radically altered institutional arrangements we will develop to advance community library service? The learning system developed for community library service will, of necessity, make more systematic utilization of the common motivational experience provided by radio, television, and film. These media are very successful at providing motivational experiences. They turn people on. Yes, you learn a few facts from television and film, you learn a few concepts, but basically these are motivational media, and once a person has had this motivational experience, there ought to be some systematic arrangement in schools and in libraries for people to get together and reinforce these experiences. Opportunities are needed for learners of all ages to gather in small groups for reaction discussions with competent people available to help them. Such sessions should be scheduled in schools and libraries.

What I am really trying to lead up to as a final comment is that nothing will come from the discussions at this conference unless the professionals involved here take the lead in developing a new approach. When are we going to get rid of all these separate boards, these separate administrations, these separate governing boards that control museums, libraries, parks, schools, etc.? Until somebody comes up with community coordination in the form of a community director and board of learning resources, conferences of this type will be a pleasant experience and nothing more. I am not the first person to propose this, by any means. Floyd Reece many years ago advocated a superintendent of education. His mistake was in terminology, because with such a title, the concept is limited to schools. Let's forget the past. Under this community director of learning resources should come schools, churches, educational institutions, museums, libraries, everything in the community that has an educational program or a collection of educational resources. All of these need to be coordinated, so that the financial resources of the community can be justly and wisely allocated.

Someone will immediately say that this is merely adding bureaucracy to bureaucracy, that the job is too big to be done by one coordinator or by one coordinating board. So let's have regional and subregional resource boards. We have given up too easily on these subregional units for school control just because they didn't work out in the first year. We always try something for one year and, if it doesn't work, we forget about it. Well, with even the simplest change in education, you had better think of a minimum five-year program to begin. Change comes very slowly and comes with difficulty. Forget everything else I have said, but let us go out of this conference with the determination to achieve some sort of coordination in learning resources on the community level. If not, we will spend another century having meetings, talking about the development of community library service, talking about how institutions can work together. One day we will have to come to the concept of a central board of learning resources, with a central coordinating staff. Unless this is done, we will never truly have a community program for continuing education, or a community program for learning resources.

NOTES

1. James S. Coleman, *Equality of Educational Opportunity* (Washington, D.C.: GPO, 1966).

2. Central Advisory Council for Education (England), *Children and Their Primary Schools* (the Plowden Report), (London: Her Majesty's Stationery Office, 1967).

3. Mark M. Krug, "The Social Studies—Search for New Directions," in *What Will Be Taught—The Next Decade*, ed. M. M. Krug (Itasca, Ill.: F. E. Peacock, 1972), p. 201.

4. Arthur W. Foshay, *Curriculum for the 1970's: An Agenda for Action* (Washington, D.C.: National Education Association, 1970), p. 67.

5. Sterling M. McMurrin, "What Tasks for the Schools?" *Saturday Review* 50:41 (Jan. 14, 1967).

6. Harold C. Wells, "To Get Beyond the Words . . .," *Educational Leadership* 28:241 (Dec. 1970).

7. Roger O. Abraham, "Cultural Differences and the Melting Pot Ideology," *Educational Leadership* 29:119 (Nov. 1971).

8. Urban Education Task Force, *Urban School Crisis: the Problem and the Solutions* (Washington, D.C.: National School Public Relations Association, 1970), p. 7.

9. James M. Cooper, "Differentiated Staffing: Some Questions and Answers," *National Elementary Principal* 41:50 (Jan. 1972).

10. Ronald C. Doll, "Alternative Forms of Schooling," *Educational Leadership* 29:391 (Feb. 1972).

11. *Ibid.*

New Directions in the Delivery of Public Services of the Community Level

Presentation:
EDMOND R. COLETTA

Response:
RODERICK G. SWARTZ

The changing nature of the economic order, along with the changing nature of social structures and attitudes, has affected the utilization of governmental activity by requiring that government assume increased and varying responsibilities. Over the last several years, all levels of government have experienced a remarkable growth in the number, complexity, and size of the programs that they have been called upon to support. We now find government supplying a multitude of varied programs and activities as the means of providing for the availability and attainment of personal well-being and advancement for its citizens. As the requirements of society become more and more complex, government faces great challenges in fulfilling social and physical needs. Consequently, the problems that government faces today are far larger and more difficult than many of those with which it has traditionally dealt.

In his book, *The Politics and Economics of State-Local Finance*, L. L. Ecker-Racz described the flow of demands as follows:

> The past, moreover, is but a foretaste of what lies ahead. Public service needs are likely to become progressively more demanding as the nation continues to grow and prosper. The reasons have been identified over and over again. The monthly increase in population is approaching 200,000; Americans live

Edmond R. Coletta is Supervising Budget Analyst, Division of Budget, State of Rhode Island, Providence, Rhode Island.

Roderick G. Swartz is Deputy Secretary, National Commission on Libraries and Information Science, Washington, D.C.

21

longer and retire earlier, thus adding to the dependent age groups; people concentrate more and more in and around cities where government must do things for them, and each public operation is costlier; continuing prosperity is whetting the public's appetite for more and better public services; business firms need improved community services to grow and to hold their own against even keener competition; political leaders regardless of party or government affiliation promise social reforms and stimulate the expectations of the less privileged; and organized demands for larger shares in national prosperity have reached a militancy new to the American experience. [1]

The extent to which a governmental program fulfills its stated objectives depends upon the degree of success which that program has (1) in deriving sufficient financial support, and (2) in positing an effective administrative capability for the management of these resources.

ACCOUNTABILITY

The goals of government are realized through the expenditure of public funds. Since resources seldom meet projected requirements, we are plagued with the problem of limited resources and the related difficulty of allocating whatever resources we do have. Unfortunately, there are no easy answers in the setting of priorities; there is no scientific means of allocating resources.

Government services do not exist in a vacuum. Accordingly, success in obtaining the levels of financial support needed to attain desired goals depends on the relative value and importance of a particular program as recognized by the executive, the legislature, and the related influences of the community at large. John D. Millett, Chancellor of the Ohio Board of Regents, in addressing the problems faced by today's university in seeking increased resources, noted: "Individuals of wealth and governments which spend the tax income of their citizens will not distribute funds to an institution serving no useful social objective." [2]

What is this notion of visibility? It is extremely important that visibility flow from a positive approach of accountability for the management of governmental programs. Accountability is interpreted as an assignable, measurable responsibility for the demonstrating of results from the expenditure of public funds for governmental programs, programs designed to achieve definite goals within the constraints of legal, fiscal, and resource limitations.

The importance of accountability is found in its relationship to resource allocation, and ultimately in its influence on the delivery of services: what kind, how much, to whom, and for what duration. The past president of the American Library Association, Mrs. Lillian Bradshaw, at the annual conference of the New England Library Association in October, 1970, emphasized the need for accountability. In making a plea for recognition of the increasing demands on governmental services, Mrs. Bradshaw asked, "What does this say about our attitude toward the necessity for accountability and measurements of achievement which merit financial support? . . . What does it say should be librarians' planning toward achieving maximum value from the tax dollar?" [3]

Each of us might very well question the need for a visibility and accomplishment evaluation of our particular program. It must be recognized that, from a managerial point of view, the accountability approach has a positive benefit. Accountability is not to be construed as punitive in nature. It requires us to examine principles which have long since been accepted, but, in some instances, are no longer applicable. Notwithstanding the sensitivity of this approach, we must think very "hard" about what we are really up to. Too often we are misled into believing that we are accomplishing our basic mission because we are performing our functions effectively and efficiently; just because we perform a function well does not necessarily justify the continuation of that function.

ALLOCATION OF RESOURCES

The demands generated by contemporary society in all its elements, coupled with the new voices from various age groups and special clientele, have placed considerable strain on the traditional processes of resource allocation, indeed challenging the very basic concepts underlying these processes. No longer can we merely rely on what has been done before as justification for adding to or even continuing governmental effort. No longer can we expect artificial divisions of organization to correspond to the functional responsibility of government to meet social needs. No longer can we afford to view governmental programs as unrelated or atomistic activities, thereby ignoring the potential benefits that can be realized by considering such activities under a total systems concept.

As a description of the shortcomings in the current budgetary process, the before-mentioned deficiencies serve to point toward an approach which can serve as a sound basis for the rational allocation of resources. Since there is never enough money to finance all programs, we must develop better mechanisms for allocating funds wisely and effectively. What we need are technologies for making better decisions, technologies recognizing more systematic, comprehensive, sophisticated ways for improving decision-making. Are such processes possible? Can we construct an approach by which it is possible to determine which demands are better than others? Can we move from an approach which is incremental, fragmented, and representative of special needs to one that emphasizes accomplishment, effectiveness, and accountability? Can we ever expect to know how to invest scarce resources so as to attain the greatest return in program benefits?

One cannot conceive of a more ideal situation than seeking and obtaining funds from an inexhaustible spring simply on the basis of articulating need, devising programs to meet that need, and demonstrating an improvement in the degree of fulfilling that need. Yet, while all of these steps are necessary in justifying financial support, requests for funding a particular program must be viewed within the context of all requests. Utilizing this perspective, each request is seen as competing for scarce resources with an endless list of diverse programs, each of which is, clearly, just as important as the others.

We are all mindful of the difficult financial problems confronting government today. Over the last several years, state and local governments especially have been faced with increasing costs, particularly with open-ended programs, coupled with the inability of revenue structures to keep pace with increasing expenditures. As a general rule, tax collections from existing established sources tend to grow at one and one-half the rate of expenditures. The difference is principally achieved by raising tax rates or instituting new taxes, a most formidable task in a tax-conscious society. As an alternative to raising new revenue, an often-heard mandate is the community's demand to "live" within existing resources, and the competition for resources becomes even keener. This is the real world today.

MANAGEMENT OF PUBLIC SERVICES

The delivery of public services is a function of the interrelationship between extant public needs and the processes underlying the governmental operations attempting to fulfill those needs. In practice, public services take their direction from pressures from within the community and, more importantly, from the influences of the administrative hierarchy. To admit that governmental services are provided only within a need-supply framework is to ignore the direct and indirect roles of the entire governmental structure.

The processes underlying the obtaining of resources and the planning for maximum utilization of those resources are so interrelated as to suggest an approach which visualizes each as flowing from the other. This becomes possible by developing budgeting processes which provide for the linking of resource expenditures to initial sound program planning.

The assumption, basic to improved budgeting processes, is that most human beings are rational, and therefore will make better decisions if they are given better information. Better information can evolve through the use of a systematic approach to decision-making, one which provides for a uniform and regular analytic capability at key points of the government's decision-making process, particularly the budget process. The primary objective of such a approach is to incorporate analysis as a regular method in the budgetary process. The current attempt to achieve this methodology in the budgeting field is known as a planning programming budgeting system, or PPBS.

DELIVERY OF PUBLIC SERVICES

Because PPBS has its roots in the budgetary process, it is often attacked on the basis that its purpose is mainly directed toward the better allocation of resources. This position detracts substantially from the potential of an effective PPB system in the improvement of the delivery of public services. While it is true that we, as central administrators, are seeking a better mechanism for allocating resources, it is logical to assume that the attainment of this end will result from a *uniformly improved decision-making process* throughout all government. This is our objective.

Consider the need for an overall improved management capability. If we are to keep pace with the increasingly difficult problems that government faces today, we must improve our management of governmental programs. PPBS has as its purpose an approach toward this end by offering program administrators a methodology to improve their ability to manage governmental programs by making better decisions. It is my contention that the effectiveness of service rendered is a direct result of the degree of analysis conducted by program administrators. Quality analysis, through PPBS, is the key to improved decision-making.

All of us in the governmental sector are troubled these days by the lack of cohesive effort among federal, state, and local governments. It is possible to find within a particular program a multiplicity of effort divided not only on a vertical functional basis among these three governmental levels, but also horizontally, among differing agencies within the same governmental jurisdiction.

In some instances, funding requirements are so complicated that we often marvel at the ability of our program administrators to derive funds successfully in order to provide services. We find a variety of funding requirements and restrictions depending first, on what program objective is being sought, and second, on which governmental jurisdiction is funding the program. Whereas some program requirements speak of maintaining previous levels of effort, others are obviously less concerned with additive effort and permit the receiving governmental jurisdiction to use the grant as replacement for its own funds. While some programs require the participating government to support programs with actual financial participation, thereby adding to the overall level of service, other programs very simply require in-kind matching, or even more. Some recognize simply and solely the presence of need. The types of requirements and possible combinations are innumerable. Suffice it to say that uniformity is nonexistent either (1) as among differing governmental levels, or (2) as within the same governmental jurisdiction. It is readily apparent from the previous examples that the interrelationships and variables between funding and delivery of services are important.

Moreover, program services can be fragmented among a host of governmental agencies. One example of such fragmentation can be found in state-wide programs of employment resources and welfare administration. Notwithstanding the importance of the public sector's efforts in this critical area, it is not unusual to find in a state a host of governmental agencies, each directed toward the same objective. It is not unlikely to find the efforts of these governmental agencies so little coordinated with one another as to speak, perhaps, of duplicated or segmented effort.

Consider the effect of all this fragmentation and duplicity of effort on the citizen who is, after all, the taxpayer. He must be concerned when encountering duplication of effort and waste of valuable resources. When confronted with allegations of wasted effort, we may indeed have difficulty in justifying our efforts. How can we justify that which we have difficulty in understanding?

How can we properly define objectives, when the source of service may be under several types of auspices? How can we define need, when so much of what should be obtained is not even desired? How can we integrate the interrelationships between major program areas? How do the relationships of differing levels of government affect any single program?

Definitely, we must unite our efforts and reconcile our goals, so that the total effort makes sense. Unless all this diffusion of energy

—thinking, planning, and activating—is pulled together in a logical and coherent manner, we are not going to fulfill our responsibilities in meeting needs. PPBS forces us to think of needs within a total systems approach. The overall system must be viewed on a useful approach. If this is the way to go, how do we get there?

PLANNING PROGRAMMING BUDGETING

PPBS is a program budgeting system which integrates planning, programming, and budgeting into a unified, continuous, and comprehensive process. Its major purpose is to provide decision makers with a highly analytic approach for the better allocation of resources. It is a formalized process which provides for determining goals and objectives thereto, and for the selection, from among a range of alternative programs, of that one alternative considered most effective and efficient in the attainment of a specified objective. Simply put, it employs a systematic approach that identifies program objectives and measures program accomplishment. This approach requires a clear statement of goals and a structure of programs directed toward achievement of such goals.

Admittedly, there are those who pose the pertinent question as to whether this approach is indeed possible for social assistance, health, and education programs, where goals are multidimensional, few objective measures of achievement exist, and where no satisfactory definition of standards has been identified, either quantitatively or qualitatively. Can these particular types of governmental programs be separated and defined in such a way that effectiveness can be measured?

Goal setting and the definition of clear-cut objectives are not simple processes in the social fields. Indeed, we have found them very difficult. In a democracy, the philosophy of equal opportunity demands that we think in terms of service to all. Yet in the field of education, especially in the library segment thereof, programs generally revolve around closely defined clientele. This presents a challenge that is far from being adequately met. Should we be concerned with those who are in need of service but who have not come forward to seek it? Should we endeavor to provide increasingly higher quality and specified programs for those making demands on the service? Or are we speaking of a combination of these services? Quite obviously, before we can invest very scarce resources so as to attain the greatest benefits, we must have already clearly identified and set our goals and objectives. This means that, in the field of education, prior to the development of programs of implementation, we must address ourselves in a realistic manner as to what man's educational needs are in our society today. In this sense, does not the fundamental issue revolve around a determination of what man should know and be able to do as a result of that knowledge? I submit that we must ask the right questions on the correct plane and in the proper sequence, from goals to objectives and activities, and from broad directions of government to specific needs and program ends. We must think very "hard" about what we are really up to.

Once the need has been established and a specific objective defined, PPBS requires us to select from a range of alternative programs the most effective and efficient alternative leading to the attainment of the specific objective. In order to assess properly each alternative, we must be in a position to measure its impact on the intended objective. This process requires the setting of indicators which evaluate and measure program success in a meaningful way. While service or volume indicators serve a useful purpose as quantitative measures of output, they cannot be used directly to measure program achievement. Impact indicators, on the whole, consider the interrelationship of quantitative and qualitative outputs in terms of the stated objective. Simply put, we are seeking answers to what will determine success and how we can evaluate the progress that is being made toward achieving end objectives.

As I indicated before, these tasks are surely difficult, yet not unattainable. My optimism is founded upon consciousness of those resources which are the very core of program administration—the professionals in the field. Who would better relate to the highly sophisticated relationships demanded in analysis than those actually managing the programs? I submit that, given sufficient time, direction, and a reliable methodology, professional program administrators can successfully perform the analysis of which I have been speaking.

One of my most rewarding experiences in developing our analytic program budgeting system in Rhode Island occurred during an educational seminar for departmental and agency personnel on the theory, techniques, and application of PPBS. In the last stages of the seminar, we asked the participants, in small study groups, to apply what they had learned of PPBS to an area in which they were presently working. A group of professionals in a major state program reviewed a specific program element currently operative in the state's health delivery system. It was interesting to note the manner in which the group attacked the problem.

At first, the group evinced some hesitancy which seemed to be related more to the prospective visibility of that program than to a lack of confidence in their knowledge of PPBS methodology. Apparently, once the group performed some substantive analysis, it became evident to them that a continuation of the study would necessarily require the raising of some basic issues regarding the fundamental value of the program. It was at this point that, instead of resisting or even curtailing the study, the group became deeply immersed in the problem. This is important to me. It demonstrates that, notwithstanding the real possibility of some adverse conclusions, this group chose to study the problem on a positive note. Admittedly, I had expected no less. It confirmed my expectations that a group of professionals, upon discovering some critical problems within their programs, would immediately seek proper remedies. This experience suggests that, given an opportunity to examine a program critically, concerned administrators will not avoid visibility and all its ramifications. I was pleased that in this instance the program analysis approach was successful in (1) suggesting that area of review, (2) in providing a mechanism for analysis, and (3) in sustaining the interest of the group, because its members knew that their conclusions, rather than finding an ultimate rest on a shelf in some back room, would be used to the benefit of their program. This last point is vital to the successful implementation of a PPB system.

If the conclusions of a study are to find application, then we in central positions must fulfill our roles at this stage of the process. We must either permit adequate flexibility for program administrators to properly implement positive results, and/or provide the additive means and support to accomplish those ends. We cannot pay lip service to agency analysis. How can we ask program administrators to perform quality analysis and then, by either action or inaction on our part, withhold support of the study results? Such would not be in the interests of effective governmental administration. We endorse analysis. Indeed, we welcome every opportunity to utilize analytic bases for substantiating program changes.

Obviously, I must be concerned, in the last analysis, with improvements in the delivery of public services. However, my immediate concern is to provide the basic methodological approach capable of generating these improvements. If innovation connotes change for improvement in the management and delivery of public services, then this is my goal—innovation through analysis.

My objective, then, is the institution of systematic, high quality analysis at key points in the decision-making process. Sound analysis should be the foundation of any program change, whether it be a minor incremental shift, a quantum jump, an introduction of new concepts of planning and funding, or even the complete scrapping of an existing program.

Because PPBS fundamentally considers programs under a total

systems concept, it thereby requires an evaluation of the impact and relationship of complementary programs having the same basic objectives. This factor has great significance. It demands that administrators consider coordinated and cooperative measures as integral and essential components of any proposed alternative. When I say that some kind of coordination and cooperation among programs is imperative, you must realize that I speak of this with the qualification that, although it may be far from easy, it is possible. Indeed, in Rhode Island, in the field of library services, the kinds of cooperation that are evolving after some years of effort, following a new state law, run counter to the grain and are to be admired in the light of the leadership and immense effort that the programs reflect, as well as for the improved service they are attaining.

The future of improved decision-making is not in the hands of those at the central staff level of government. The means for achieving this end exists throughout the governmental bureaucracy. I have every reason to believe the ability is present. We need energy, creativeness, dedication, and leadership.

NOTES

1. L. L. Ecker-Racz, *The Politics and Economics of State-Local Finance.* (Englewood Cliffs, N.J.: Prentice-Hall, 1970), pp. 195-96.

2. John D. Miller, "Higher Education's Contribution," *Compact* 4:25 (Oct. 1970).

3. Lillian M. Bradshaw, "ALA's President Describes . . . A New Order of Things," *New England Library Association Newsletter* 7:67 (Dec. 1970).

Response | Mr. Swartz

Mr. Coletta has given us a background paper which outlines various innovative management techniques used to bring general community services to the public. In essence, he has hit us with a block buster of an innovation—PPBS, touched lightly on several other areas which could have used amplification, and perhaps unintentionally overlooked a couple of other major areas. I would like to comment on each of these areas and attempt to relate each of them to the delivery of information services to the community.

First, let us look at the innovative technique of PPBS. As an economist and budget analyst, Mr. Coletta made a plea for the adoption of this technique. He makes a strong point of relating PPBS to a "uniformly improved decision-making process." He sees it as a tool to improve this process by challenging old concepts and helping to create new goals.

But perhaps the paper stops where the really difficult answers are required. First, what is educational accountability? How does this relate to accountability in libraries? How is it possible to apply PPBS to information and library services? One must realize there is a vast difference in developing PPBS as a management tool and in securing the acceptance of PPBS as a total way of life within an organization. Many librarians who are trying to adapt to PPBS are finding the attempt time consuming and frustrating, to say the least.

Secondly, and as a corollary, it must be remembered that PPBS is only a tool—and one tool among many—for making improvements within the policy-making system. More important is the need for new ideas, clear objectives and innovations. William Summers, writing in *American Libraries*, points out that the major problem in implementing PPBS in libraries and information centers is the difficulty of determining performance objectives. [1] This difficulty, that of determining goals and objectives, is certainly amplified when we are trying to coordinate several different community information agencies with varying patterns of service. While PPBS may help this process, it should not be considered to the exclusion of other tools.

Looked at in this manner, PPBS might even be considered a detrimental tool. If the major problem in implementing PPBS in libraries and information centers is the creation of objectives and goals, PPBS as a form of analysis might crush creative thinking. Doesn't analysis opt for predictable results, rather than the uncertainties of new ideas?

COMMUNITY INVOLVEMENT

The author briefly touches on another major innovation in the delivery of public services, when he comments that "demands generated by contemporary society in all its elements and with new voices . . . have placed considerable strain on traditional resource allocation." At this point, I feel he really understates a major trend which is affecting the implementation of all public services: the involvement of the total community in the planning of its service pattern and content.

Ever since the Economic Opportunity Act of 1964 urged "maximum feasible participation," there has been an extensive effort to bring those being affected into the planning of the programs which affect them. At the national level, total community involvement is required in most federal programs. Each Model Cities neighborhood, for instance, is divided into areas and each area has its community action group. Similar activity is being generated at the local level, where citizen groups are being asked to advise and counsel with police, park, and other local agencies.

A corollary of this movement toward citizen participation has been the decentralization of authority and government. Several federal agencies have dispersed their agencies to regional centers throughout the United States. And in every sizeable community there has been a move toward some type of neighborhood community action center, where various types of community public service are available within the neighborhood.

This trend toward participation has also expressed itself inside the public organization. For example, there has been a move to involve a greater number of the staff in the decision-making process. The task force concept, or the participation of more people in the decision-making process, is again seen at all levels. Task forces were initiated by the White House prior to John F. Kennedy's inauguration. Lyndon Johnson made extensive use of the concept—for instance, the 1964 Gardner task force on education and the 1964 Wood task force on housing. One now sees participatory administration in most phases of public administration, in which all levels of personnel are involved in the decision-making process.

Within these innovative techniques being used to bring new patterns of service to the community—i.e., community involvement, participatory administration and decentralization—one can see again, just as with PPBS, many problems in implementation. The concept of participatory administration is being called into question by some critics. Herbert Wilcox, writing in the January/February, 1969, issue of *Public Administration Review* states that "the participative theorists argue that the way to achieve democratic and human values in organization is to summon up the faith that these can be created through interpersonal relationships." Sensitivity trainers, says Wilcox, "might be able to create momentarily for a small group 'a little bit of heaven' where authenticity and trust reign, but there would be a need for intermittently resensitizing the group." [2] Criticism of the participatory process from another angle was aimed at the Presidential task forces, where it was said the task forces tend to pull things together, rather than to come up with new ideas.

Along this same line others see the decentralization pattern as only a temporary expedient. Certainly decentralization will bring the services closer to the client, but differences will appear which will probably bring the reaction of centralization.

CROSSING INSTITUTIONAL LINES

Coletta touches on another major innovation when he comments that, "No longer can we afford to view governmental programs as unrelated or atomistic activities ignoring the potential benefits . . . under a total system concept." I believe he is voicing what many others are urging today, that the service itself is most important, that we have to look beyond the institution from which it now originates, and determine the best pattern for the service to reach the public.

A mild form of this development is seen in the efforts to extend services beyond the doors of the institution. Creating a "go structure" as opposed to a "come structure" has been the effort in governmental agencies, churches, and many other service agencies.

Another moderate effort in this direction is the growth of cooperative efforts among public agencies. Park departments are cooperating with police departments, libraries are cooperating with a multiplicity of agencies. All this in an effort to extend service beyond institutional boundaries.

Frustrations in many of these endeavors have caused an even more radical departure in attempting to separate service patterns from the institution itself. In some cases, professionals are almost advocating the complete overhaul of the institution if it is to improve service to the client. As Coletta says: "Just because we perform a function well does not necessarily justify the continuation of that function."

This trend of looking beyond your own institution in developing new service patterns is an important one. I can only add that it seems we quickly get caught up again in institutional bricks and mortar, even with innovative service patterns. For instance, the innovative school design of placing the learning center in the center of a building is certainly a real hazard when talking about school/public library relationships.

EFFECT ON ADMINISTRATORS AND PROFESSIONALS

In another area, I believe Mr. Coletta overlooks an important factor: the effect of these changes on the people involved in the distribution of community services. All of these moves—the instigation of PPBS, the involvement of citizen groups, participatory administration, the decentralization of power, extension of service patterns—have had a strong effect upon the professional administrator. Many public agency heads have been frightened by the more intensive participation with groups and individuals that these new tools require. Many see this participation as a restriction of professional judgment.

Often the professional feels that he, and he alone, is in the best position to know, understand, and select the best means of accomplishing the objectives of his organization. In many cases this has resulted in a severe lack of involvement with these newer tools. In a recent survey on participatory administration made by one of my students at the University of Oklahoma, he could find only four public libraries in the country which were actively and sincerely involving their staffs in a real participatory effort.

This is an area in community service patterns in which research needs to be done. We know little about how the top administrator—whether it be the U.S. President, the president of a university, the high school principal, or the director of a public library—how this administrator makes his decisions, especially if he opts to ignore this newer tool.

Coupled with this reluctant administrator is the young "firing line" professional. Almost every community agency which is staffed with professional personnel is experiencing a regeneration of real devotion to the client by the professional on the firing line. He sees himself as a person responding to the human needs of another individual, and is responding in a very personal and total fashion. Unfortunately, in many cases the firing line professional sees only the traditional client, and is slow to move out to new groups or new types of services. The staff of a large Southwest public library system was recently studied by a sociologist regarding their attitudes to a series of open forum programs financed by a national agency. Reaction from the firing line professional ranged from negative response to a more cautious positive approval—an approval that still insisted that involvement with this type of program took them away from the "real"work, i.e., traditional services to the traditional client.

All of these innovative service patterns will not work unless there is a responsive group of professionals who are educated to be ready, willing and able to experiment with innovation. In fact, as we have seen there are critics of all these techniques. Eventually these tools will probably be replaced with other, even more up-to-date techniques. It seems to me that the crucial problem in the search for new ways to provide community services is not the latest tool or technique, as much as the training of professionals for all levels, professionals who are creative, innovative, and willing to experiment.

NOTES

1. William F. Summers, "A Change in Budgetary Thinking," *American Libraries* 2:1177 (Dec. 1971).
2. Herbert G. Wilcox, "Hierarchy, Human Nature, and the Participative Panacea," *Public Administration Review* 29:61 (Jan./Feb. 1969).

Man and Media: The Library

Presentation:
GERALD R. BRONG

Response:
ROBERT HEINICH

The future of library service in our country rests on our ability to pull all of the library service elements now operating together into a system. Library roles are changing, as are the roles of all other social or service agencies. Pressures are forcing us to make better use of the monies provided for library operation; increased pressures are brought to bear as expansion of services is requested, and expected. And, in many cases, we are suddenly being held accountable for the programs we operate. This is an exciting time for library development, and a critical time.

Today the variety of library services is quite wide, and the quality is quite variable. Services are provided through school libraries or resource centers, public libraries, academic or research libraries, and special libraries. When examining the range of library services in a community, it quickly becomes apparent that there are many instances when services are duplicated between libraries, or that services are lacking. In most instances there are library service elements that serve one patron group in a community, while other patron groups in the same community are denied services by that same library element.

The quality of library service provided by any element in the library service chain is most difficult to determine. The formulation of qualitative measures for evaluating library programs is lacking. Many users of libraries, and many professionals in the library infor-

Gerald R. Brong is Assistant Director, Audiovisual Center, Washington State University, Pullman, Washington.

Robert Heinich is Professor of Education, Audiovisual Center, Indiana University, Bloomington, Indiana.

mation field, are very critical of the quality of library service provided within our country. Some indicate that the present condition of library service is so poor that all existing library service elements should be eliminated and new service elements put into operation. This debate will be avoided in this paper, but one assumption about the services available from today's libraries will be made—the services tomorrow can, and must, be improved. In libraries, the most useful information locating tools have been developed in fields which the frequency of demand justified the production of the tool (i.e., indices, abstracts, data sheets, information handling machines, etc.) or where society has recognized a need and demanded the tool. [1] The same phenomenon will take place with the provision of total library service.

This paper reviews developments in the library technology field, as represented by the continued development of nonprint media, audiovisual technology, and their application. One of the new technologies briefly discussed is the technology of instruction. The library is viewed as an active element in the total teaching-learning system serving our society. In 1968, Herbert Ostrach described the school of the future by stating:

> One need only open the newspaper to learn what the school of the future will be like. We read of multimedia libraries from which students will select materials with a computer and sophisticated teaching machines into which whole courses will be programmed. In the newspaper articles I have read it is also assumed that the physical structure and the scheduling function of the school will also radically change. [2]

Predictions about tomorrow's libraries abound in the literature. Ostrach goes on to question the rationale of these plans for the school of tomorrow—the rationale might be based on the plans of the educational hardware industry (or software industry) to provide or sell new teaching-learning resources, rather than the plans of the educators operating the schools or the users of the schools. [3] The same can be said about libraries.

The parallels that can be drawn between schools and libraries are many. Henry Brickell, when he was describing a method for organizing the New York State schools for educational change in 1961, stated:

> A school, like any other institution, tends to continue doing what it was established to do, holding itself relatively stable and resisting attempts at restructuring. . . . Stability in the

institutional structure makes for maximum output of the
results the structure was designed to produce. [4]

Stability in an institution which helps insure high output is fine, if
the products of that output of today are acceptable tomorrow. The
products or services of our institutions change as the patrons served
change. Libraries as institutions, and the personnel staffing libraries,
resist change. When change takes place we describe it as innovation.

In libraries, as well as in other areas of endeavor, there are two
types of innovation. First is the innovation found by creating a new
product or service. Second, and most common in libraries today, is
innovation in the methodology employed to produce the product or
provide the service. [5] Planning for the operation of libraries is, therefore, based on the identification of the successful innovations in the
library/learning center field, plus the defined goals for the operation
of the libraries.

If the librarian can be thought of as a set of functions rather than
a person, we can describe the function of the librarian as the interface between the universe of stored information and the application
of that information. [6] The librarian (and the library) of tomorrow
will bring the information, regardless of storage format or storage
location, together with the requestor of that information. In addition, the librarian, whose activities are supported by the library,
will become actively involved in the actual utilization of the information obtained. The school library will serve the general public; the
academic library will support special requests of the grade school
learner; public libraries will provide a full curriculum of educational
experiences; libraries will be dynamic institutions meeting expressed needs of society.

Before exploring the implications of audiovisual technology in
libraries, it may be helpful to attach meaning to a few words or concepts to be discussed. In defining the college library, and this definition is applicable to most types of libraries, Don Ely says, "LI-
BRARY—A FUNCTION (not a place) WHOSE RESPONSIBILITY
IS TO SYSTEMATICALLY (there must be a plan acquisition related to the needs of the institution to which it is attached) COL-
LECT INFORMATION (information is used to include realia and
nonbook materials), CLASSIFY IT (the system must recognize the
requirements of the retrieval system), STORE IT (storage for retrieval purposes may require conversion to appropriate forms)
AND, UPON DEMAND (the act of identifying existence of a unit
of information must be efficient and systematic) RETRIEVE IT
AND ASSIST IN ADAPTING IT TO THE USE TO BE MADE OF
THE INFORMATION." [7] Ely's definition of a library, as used in
this paper, implies that a library collects information which may be

stored in print or nonprint form, i.e., motion pictures, slide sets, audio recordings, etc. Further, libraries are actively involved in the utilization of the information by the patron. We shall consider libraries as an element in an active teaching-learning system, both in and out of the school.

Library collections consist of informational units. An informational unit is a device or thing which contains information and presents that information when needed. Media, on the other hand, should be thought of not as a fixed characteristic or a class of materials but an operational term applied to any of man's extensions of himself— whether they are words, films, books, paintings, or other recordings of information. [8] Audiovisual resources are those resources that are not dependent on the printed word to provide their information. Usually these resources include motion pictures, audio recordings, still pictures, realia, or combinations of media.

Library patrons are users of the library services. These may be individuals as well as institutions. Patrons may seek information for recreational purposes, for learning, or for the solution to a problem. The use of the information causes behavior that may be affected by the information obtained. In some cases the information used is retained and we say "learned," but frequently it is forgotten. As libraries play a role in "teaching" or in passing on "learning," they become educational institutions and the processes of instructional technology will come into play.

"Teaching is any imparting of information that leads to learning; instruction is the imparting of *ordered* information." [9] Teaching strategy is the designing of an educational process or environment based on identified objectives that will lead the learner to a defined behavior goal. [10] The process of developing a set of systematic techniques, using necessary resources to achieve defined objectives with the learner, can be thought of as instructional technology.

Circulation or delivery systems employed by libraries are the mechanisms that provide the patron access to the desired information. Circulation systems move the informational unit from one place to another. The merging of the concept of circulation and delivery systems begins to make it difficult to differentiate between circulation and display. If we combine the two concepts we have a circulation/display system. This system provides access to, and display of, the stored information in the library's collection.

THE NEW TECHNOLOGIES

The six-year-old of today possesses a great deal of information even before he enters our formalized educational system. By the time many six-year-olds have entered school, they have spent 4,000 hours in front of the television set. By the time this same child graduates from high school, he will have clocked some 15,000 hours of cartoons, violence, sex, commercials, and something we call educational television.[11] The cliché may be overworn, but one of the major revolutions of the 70s will undoubtedly be the communications revolution. This expansion of the communications spectrum from print to sound and image is having a massive impact on the institution we have named the library.[12] The technologies having the most impact on libraries are: (1) technologies of information storage, (2) technologies allowing for the production of informational units, (3) technologies allowing new ways of information delivery, and (4) instructional technology.

Libraries are becoming huge mechanisms for identifying what information is wanted, reproducing or providing the information from storage, and providing the patrons with a freedom of interaction with the information. It is evident that these new technologies are transporting us from a time of scarcities of information materials to a time where increased selectivity is essential.[13]

In the library of tomorrow, and frequently in the library of today, when we speak of "book" we are making reference to the generic idea of book—the concept has been broadened to all sources of information storage.[14] Nonprint material can be handled in the library, except for physical storage, like print materials. The catalog of the library's holdings will catalog the information available through the library system rather than physical information storage devices. For using nonprint materials, the patron will frequently require some sort of a display device in order to access or obtain the information from the storage medium.

With the increased use of nonprint media resources, libraries suddenly became involved with a host of problems that need to be solved. There is the incompatibility of materials formats with various display devices; pricing of nonprint materials continues to cover the full range from inexpensive to extremely expensive, and frequently there is little relationship between the cost of the informational materials and their value; distribution of nonprint materials, in many cases, continues to be a haphazard procedure when compared with the print materials; and, as with anything new, if nonprint materials can be classified as new, there is the hazard of "bandwagonism." In 1968, during a faculty development institute in educational media at San Jose State College, Richard Lewis, then of the San Jose State College faculty, pointed out that only a few of the supposed media innovations being presented today cannot be taken care of with the techniques and equipment that have been around for some time. New types of hardware, and frequently materials, have the power to attract zealous supporters. New hardware devices have a kind of emotional appeal; this appeal is often without much rationality. As a consequence, the introduction of new hardware or materials formats is usually followed by a number of people who seize upon it with great enthusiasm, and proceed to apply it to a whole host of social concerns with only the flimsiest of rationales. 15

New technologies of information storage will provide increased access to a wider variety of information. People unable to obtain or use information from print materials will be able to access information from nonprint. Democratization of information access may be closer to realization with the increased use of the nonprint information sources. The library of tomorrow will not be a true information center, if indeed that is its goal, if the informational resources available are limited to print materials. This increased access to informational resources will lead to an increased use of the new technologies for the communication of ideas. Libraries will become involved in creating new informational resources. The technologies allowing for the production of nonprint resources by libraries, or the users of libraries, could have as much impact on the recording and distribution of man's knowledge as the invention of the printing press. With the use of our new technologies, it is now possible to record the sights, sounds, sensations, emotions, and impact of today's society. Technology has increased the simplicity through which mechanical/electrical devices can be used to record events. The miniaturization of information recording and display devices and the reduction in costs of these instruments increases the probability of use. Libraries now check out all sorts of information storage units and the appropriate display devices; tomorrow they will be checking out the devices that allow the generation of new informational storage units such as audio recorders, cameras, video tape recorders, or computer manipulation devices.

Libraries operating as information centers could become centers for full manipulation of stored information. Libraries rent typewriters by the hour, and they can rent other information manipulation devices. For example, in the February, 1972, issue of *American Libraries*, in the "Of Note" column on page 103, a newsclip indicates that the Monterey, California, library provides access to computer services through a coin-operated terminal. A patron may purchase two and one-half minutes of computer time on a Hewlett Packard 9100A Computer for 25 cents. Today that same patron can buy Xerox copies of printed materials in coin-operated machines, and, in some cases, duplications of audio recordings can be obtained through coin-operated devices. Through the use of technology, whether the technology requires the use of a coin or not, information duplication and processing, along with new information generation, is becoming a part of the role of the library.

Advances in telecommunications technology might be the most promising technological innovation available to libraries. Audiovisual materials lend themselves to electronic distribution. Decisions in the late 60s and early 70s by the Federal Communications Commission, encouraging the expansion of independent common carriers, undoubtedly had a major effect on the reducing of data transmission costs over long lines operated by Western Union, American Telephone and Telegraph, and the independent carriers.[16] The development of national library networks using data transmission capabilities has been enhanced by this turn of events. The Conference on Interlibrary Communications and Information Networks, held in September, 1970, stands out as one of the milestones in the interlibrary communication/management field. The proceedings of that conference have been published, under the editorship of Joseph Becker, by the American Library Association. A follow-up on that conference will be held as a preconference session prior to the July, 1972, ALA conference in Chicago. It became clear during the 1970 Conference that the movement of information between libraries, and between libraries and patrons, was a top priority to be faced in this country. Most discussions today about library networking and electronic distribution of information are concerned with information movement between libraries. Tomorrow we have the capability of moving information from the library to the patron, wherever the patron might be, in addition to interlibrary information transfer.

At Washington State University, audio and video information is distributed from the library to patrons upon request. A patron anywhere with access to a telephone may dial the Listening Library and enter into a reference negotiation process with the library attendant. Once the audio item desired has been selected, it can be transmitted to the requestor by normal telephone lines or, if the patron is in Pullman and should desire, the same audio material may be transmitted to him on an FM radio channel. Patrons may also request a display of video materials on campus or in their homes with the origination point being the library. The delivery system used for the FM Broadcast or video delivery is the privately owned community antenna television (CATV) system; this system also provides off-air commercial television and educational television broadcasts to the populace of the city. Brigitte Kenney, Chairwoman of the American Library Association Information Systems Automation Division Telecommunications Committee, and Frank Norwood, Executive Director of the Joint Council on Educational Telecommunications, have stated, "We believe that CATV will become perhaps *the* most important means for interconnecting libraries, as well as for connecting users to libraries." [17]

We are experiencing a communication revolution. If it is not a revolution, it is a rather rapid evolutionary condition. New methods of storing and displaying information, new methods of information circulation and delivery, new ways to use information to achieve defined objectives, and new ways of producing informational units to communicate with others is bound to have an impact on libraries. The impact will occur even if no definitive action is taken by the managers of library or information collections. Rather than waiting for the impact, it would be profitable to design for the new communication tools and methodology, to be ready to apply the new technologies, and to provide leadership in applying these technologies to improve the welfare of the patron group, or society as a whole, served by the libraries. One fact is becoming clear as the designing for new technologies takes place—the precise role of specific library types (academic, school, public, research, government, etc.), as compared to other types, is becoming unclear.

An example of how these new technologies might affect libraries can be seen in the planning for the ATS-F project. Systems developed for communication need to be two-way. Not only must the information flow from the information center to the recipient, but the recipient needs to be able to communicate back to, or control the information presenting device. This is true for library communication systems. In May, 1973, the Applications Technology Satellite-F will be launched. Shortly following this launch, an experimental program demonstrating the distribution of educational television to selected areas of the Rocky Mountain states, and the Appalachian region, will commence. The key feature of this experiment will be the use of hundreds of small, low-cost earth terminals. The cost of a normal Comsat terminal is between $5 and $6 million. The terminals described for this project will have a price range from $2,000 to $5,000. A $2,000 terminal will have reception capability only, while a $5,000 terminal will have reception/transmission capability. A terminal will handle up to four video channels or the processing of a thousand or so computer digital response channels.[18] Educational television, since education is not confined to the schools, also need not be confined to the schools. Satellites will enhance the ability to communicate and educate. It appears that within the next five years, satellite centered distribution of educational television programs with several possible modes of real time student response measurement is technically feasible and commercially viable.[19] Libraries, as information centers, have a use for their new satellite technology.

Cable communications, like satellite systems, provide new ways of moving and using the information contained in libraries. In many communities and states, libraries are becoming actively involved in planning for cable communication or CATV systems. In Washington State, for example, the Washington State Advisory Council on Libraries (which reports to the Washington State Library Commission and the Washington Library Association) is involved in statewide planning for potential uses of cable communication systems. The Council is working with the state governmental agencies, exploring criteria for franchising cable systems for communities and helping municipal agencies plan for cable communication. In)ctɔber of 1971 a seminar was sponsored by the Kettering Foundation and held in Dayton, Ohio, exploring the full implications of cable communications. The Association for Educational Telecommunications, Publicable, and many other organizations are involved in attempting to reserve for educational agencies or systems, including libraries, access to the communication channels available through cable communications.

One of the most significant developments has been the defining and application of instructional technology. Within the Association for Educational Communications and Technology, and other organizations, considerable effort is being expended to define the domains of teaching and learning, and apply systems design procedures to the teaching-learning process. This has led to the development and refinement of instructional technology. No attempt will be made here to develop a detailed definition of instructional technology. It will suffice to say that the application of the principles of instructional technology is extremely significant within the library as the library becomes involved in the teaching/learning process. The application of instructional technology by the library as it designs learning experiences for patrons immediately moves the library into the role of an educational institution. As libraries develop outreach programs they are applying aspects of instructional technology. The library of tomorrow will continue to actively participate in the processes of information storage, as it does today, and information usage. As the library assumes a role of assisting with information use, information processing, teaching-learning, or the creation of new informational storage units, it will call upon the nonprint information technologies.

MANAGEMENT FOR SERVICE

If we accept the premise that one of the primary goals of librarianship is the extension of library services to meet the needs and desires of all the population, we need to:

1. Design management systems allowing us to acquire needed informational units and to enter these units into our collection in an orderly retrievable manner.

2. Operate bibliographic control systems that will facilitate the cataloging of the information contained in our collection and assist in the retrieving of that information.
3. Develop systems to allow for the display of a wide variety of informational storage mediums.
4. Design staffing patterns that will provide a team of specialists to assist the library patron in accessing, and more importantly, utilizing the stored information.
5. Operate a management system that forces evaluation of existing operations and planning of methods to improve total library service.

The key is management. Management is the application of resources (personnel, administrative authority, financial capability and control, communications, planning, and holdings in the collection) to meet the defined objectives of the library program. Management is the nitty-gritty that keeps the ongoing program functioning.

OBJECTIVES

Formulation and Program Design

A program needs to exist for a purpose, and defined objectives provide a statement of that purpose. Objective formation today must be cognizant of the current ferment caused by developments in the fields of nonbook information transfer, reprography, miniaturization, and automation. [20]   With the flood of nonprint materials, collection development is critical—before collection development can commence it is essential that the decisions be made as to formats of the informational units that will be in the collection. It is not safe to say that all collections will have all varieties of materials. The collection will reflect the identified needs of the patrons to be served, as defined by the goals and objectives, in both the information provided and the methods of provision.

Programming planning for libraries, especially nonprint collections, is an essential if they are to become more than a passive warehouse filled with informational units. Library operations are made up of inconsistencies—one such inconsistency is the emphasis on expanding the collection while always increasing accessibility to the stored information. [21]   Problems of storage and display of nonprint materials are complex—nonprint materials almost always are more costly per unit than print, require more storage space or specialized storage, complex maintenance, and expensive display facilities. Decisions to provide nonprint resources must include decisions to provide display facilities—a $400, 16mm sound film requires a $500 projector.

Ongoing Program Management

The four components of the ongoing program are: selection and acquisition; bibliographic control systems; methods of providing materials for use to the patron group; and maintenance of the materials collection. The components are based on program objectives and affected by budget, personnel, and patron service.

Selection and Acquisition may be considered together, since management of the processes involved may be intertwined. In selecting the nonprint items affirmative answers to the following questions are sought: (1) is there a need for an item with this content in our library, (2) is this medium of storage and presentation suitable for the contained information and our intended purpose, (3) are techniques employed in producing the item and are its technical qualities acceptable, (4) is the content accurately presented or presented in a manner to meet our needs, (5) are there superior items available, and (6) can we afford to acquire and provide this item?

Evaluation is an important ingredient in selecting nonprint materials. Actually displaying the item and having it examined and evaluated by a group of experts is not always practical. To expedite the evaluation process review sources are used. Libraries can subscribe to commercial review services (i.e., *Landers Film Reviews*), or obtain reviews in professional literature (i.e., *Business Screen* or *Educational Screen and A V Guide*). Other tools such as the *Multi Media Reviews Index* may also be used. Purchase may be based on these reviews.

The best way to describe the purchase of nonprint materials is that it is a mystical experience understood only by a few experienced audiovisual center business managers. There is no one way to do it. There are trade-in and sales policies that are constantly changing and vary widely between companies. Distributors for items from the smaller producers frequently change (many of today's significant nonprint items come from the small independent producers), and often prices slide up and down depending on the current market. There are restrictions placed on use of the materials. Catalogs flow into audiovisual centers by the bagful, and flyers proclaim that "here is the best film on drug abuse of the century"—but with careful control of purchasing, items may be acquired that meet local needs.

Bibliographic Control Systems provide the essential element of organization for library collections. "Bibliographic" control, when we analyze the word "bibliographic," is not applicable to nonbook resources. As the term is used for other than books, it is the reference to the construct of information cataloging or control that is being made. "Bibliographic" control, as it is used here, refers to the processing of information about the information contained in the multitude of storage devices stored ready for access in the library.

For the past few decades we have heard reasons, too numerous to list here, why supposedly nonprint items could not be cataloged, classified, retrieved, provided to the patron, etc., like print informational units. Within the ALA there has been much interest in the bibliographic control of nonprint materials. The Association for Educational Communication and Technology is extending its activities in the area of applying the principles of library information science to nonprint resources and information. At the 1970 AECT convention, approval was granted to a group of nonprint librarians to form the Information Systems Division. The activities of this division will be in the standardization of bibliographic control systems and the application of library science principles to nonprint resources.

Historically, with the possible exception of the Committees on Cataloging Audiovisual Material and on Information Science, members of the AECT have tended to look on bibliographic organizational processes for nonprint media resources as logistic or high class clerical tasks. Because of this, professionals concerned with the library and information science skills necessary for the bibliographic organization and control of nonprint media have, by default, turned to professional organizations other than AECT. As recently as June 29, 1970, the Executive Committee of ALA's Cataloging and Classification Section, RTSD, unanimously passed a resolution recommending that the Canadian Library Association publication, *Non-Book Materials* (preliminary edition), be accepted as an interim guide for the cataloging of nonbook materials, with the proviso that a permanent ALA-CIA committee be established to work on any necessary revision for the final edition and its supplements. Nowhere does the motion even acknowledge the existence of the AECT. The AECT has published the revised edition of *Standards for Cataloging Nonprint Materials*. At the 1970 meeting of the American Society for Information Science, an ASIS Special Interest Group was formed to deal with problems of nonprint media and the application of information science techniques and technology to its organization and control. Through the concerted efforts of these organizations, if they acted in concert, it might be possible to solve the bibliographic control problems for nonprint resource materials.

Circulation or the Provision of Nonprint Resources to the patron is not as simple as retrieving and charging out a book. Nonprint materials nearly always require some sort of display device (projector, player, etc.), and the library might have to provide that device. If the decision is made to provide nonprint materials, provision must be made for the storage of those materials, their inspection and maintenance, and facilities and equipment for their display needs to be available. Management of the system for storing and providing nonprint materials has more complexity per single informational unit provided, or housed, than print collections.

Personnel

Looking first at the professional in the nonprint field, audiovisual specialists have been permeating the information field for many years, and finally the audiovisual specialist—who was only recently referred to as a "gadgeteer"—has almost become accepted as a professional peer with colleagues in the classroom. [22] Can we assume that he is being accepted by his library colleagues as a peer? Development of this peer relationship will be the responsibility of the audiovisual specialist. He must learn to apply the principles of library or information science to his operations with nonprint materials. He must make his skills available to librarians, helping them interact with informational stores and meet the needs of the patrons. He must become as competent as his library colleagues if he is to become a librarian.

But in managing a library today, it would not be an uncommon situation not to have an audiovisual specialist. If a management decision is made to establish an information center providing information from a wide variety of informational storage units, and if existing personnel are to manage the nonprint program, it is essential that an orientation to information, rather than a specific medium, be developed. Librarians are traditionally thought of—and operate as though it were true—as print oriented. An important fact is that librarians working with all media are involved in the process of extending the senses of man, his perceptions, and his total sensorium. [23] Library personnel serve a mediator role between information and user. The librarian becomes a translator between the patron's perception of his need for information, the identification of the true need, accessing of the information, and then provision of the information in a manner most relevant to meet the specific needs of that specific patron. As a translator, the librarian is more than the manager of the information store—he is involved in the use of information.

In addition to the professional staff, or translators, personnel need to be available to operate and maintain the electronic and mechanical devices necessary to provide display or access to the stored information in the nonprint media. Personnel skilled in inspection and repair of the informational units (film inspectors, graphic illustrator-technicians, photographic technicians) need to be available to handle physical maintenance.

Interlibrary Management (Cooperation)

Libraries have a long history of trying cooperative approaches to meeting the patron's needs. To fully develop the potentials of the nonprint materials in libraries, interlibrary cooperation or management seems essential. Management does not equate to cooperation but interlibrary management, based on cooperation between libraries with common purposes, will extend the resources available for meeting the patron's needs. For nonprint materials, interlibrary management may be given three classifications: (1) cooperative collection development, (2) bibliographic systems development and control, and (3) standardized statistical methods.

Cooperative Collection Development for nonprint materials has the same justification as for print, the procedures of identifying who develops what may be the same, and methods of cost equalization may be used for nonprint as with print resources. With print materials, interlibrary loan systems exist, and books are often shared between cooperating libraries. This is not common with nonprint materials. Interlibrary loans of a 16mm film is uncommon and audio recordings are almost never interlibrary loaned. Interlibrary management for nonprint must extend to the farthest extreme the resources available to build a collection meeting the patrons' needs—then the materials must be movable between the cooperating libraries in the interlibrary management system.

Bibliographic Systems for nonprint materials exist. Many systems. Bibliographic control systems were discussed earlier, but one management decision is essential if cooperative efforts to develop such systems are to be successful—the reinvention of the wheel must be avoided. [24] A commonality of applied bibliographic systems allowing for operation of union lists, centralized cataloging of all media, or even allowing the patron familiar in his library to use, with minimum effort, the catalog at another library is desirable and obtainable through interlibrary management. Regional bibliographic reference centers need to start providing reference services for the users of nonprint materials as they do for print.

Standardization of Statistical Methods between libraries, especially if they exist in a cooperative management environment, is highly desirable. Besides reported circulation count, registered patrons, number of items interlibrary loaned, physical description of collection, etc., there are necessary statistics associated with nonprint materials. For nonprint materials there is not now agreement as to terminology to describe or name a specific informational unit. We must standardize statistical procedures for nonprint materials. Within the AECT Information Systems Division and various AECT committees, as well as operating committees in ALA and American Society for Information Science, there are efforts under way to develop standardized terminology for the identification of the various information storage units and the transaction types that take place in an information center. To communicate between the components in the management system, a vocabulary of standardized terms is necessary—this standardized terminology and statistics are essential, and the development of methodologies to perform this evaluation function should be a high priority. Evaluation should exist as an ingredient in the planning process.

THE NETWORK—GETTING IT ALL TOGETHER

The literature abounds with definitions, or speculations, about networks that will serve libraries (some networks serve patrons of libraries, by definition). Some information scientists speculate about "The Network." The simplest definition of network suffices for our purposes: networks are systems allowing for the movement of information from one point to another. They may be electronic delivery systems (broad band cable or microwave systems) or cardboard containers used to interlibrary loan a book. With the continued use of existing networks and the development of new networks, it continues to be possible to avoid building the mega-library capable of meeting all needs. What we have is a series of libraries which, working together, can meet the needs for information.

With the increased fluidity of people as they move from place to place, from position to position, and because of the expanding population combined with the information explosion, we must create an increased fluidity of information. Information needs to flow when needed to where needed. Information on the network, not things on the network, is the key. Information may be needed to help the housewife decide on a recipe for dinner when guests are coming, and likewise information on completing a Federal income tax report may be needed by the blind man that cannot read braille. The library can provide the information. If libraries are supposed to serve all people, they need to serve all people. That concept may be simple to state, but it is complex to understand. All people include the middle class literate Americans, non-middle class literate Americans, nonliterates, handicapped, deviants, non-Americans, non-English-speaking peoples, all people. The library needs to know what is wanted by all people. If the library is to become an agency of social change it must not only meet the wants of people, it must meet their stated and un-stated needs. The network (a systematic movement of information) will increase the efficiency of information movement to the patron, and this efficiency will increase the speed with which inadequacies of the information base are discovered.

Library service requires the network. The network puts it all to-gether. It is very difficult to describe the network because it is such a simple concept, even though accomplishing the creation of the net-work is extremely complex and has defied efforts to date.

As was mentioned previously, a network is a system for providing and moving information between points. A system can be defined as a set or arrangement of things or units of service that are so connect-ed as to form an organic whole, a regular, orderly way for accom-plishing something, an ordered methodology for achieving an objec-tive. [25] There will be different networks for different purposes. The elements of the networks established will be dictated by the specific goals or objectives that are guiding the operation of the library at that moment. The network systems will be dynamic systems, chang-ing as the needs change. Management of the library system (network system) will be goal determined. The specific objectives to meet the goals will lead to a definition of the operating programs.

Our library system is fragmented into separate operating compo-nents providing specialized service to a specific clientele. These frag-ments need to be brought into a system. This is not to imply that the fragments need to be melted into a single mega-service system pro-viding information. Don Ely, in describing the contemporary college library affected by the changes of today, said that:

> I cannot accept the generalization that what is good for the college library is good for the public library or that what is good for the school library is equally desirable for the special library. There are too many types of libraries, attempting to serve too many types of audiences, to use one gross generaliza-tion about technology to cover all of them. [26]

What is needed is an opening of these service elements to use by other service elements in a library system. The basic purpose of li-braries is to provide needed information, or informational units, to a patron upon request. Working in concert, in a network, the frag-ments or elements of the library system can expand its service base.

Networking, or networks, are concepts as well as things. The pow-er of libraries in the future will be developed by networks or systems. The reader's attention is directed to the 1971 ALA publication, *Interlibrary Communication and Information Networks*, which rep-resents the proceedings of a 1970 state-of-the-art conference, for a review of networking systems as service structures. Networking is the application of a technological process to information accessing and distribution. Networks can be conceived of as technological products which have evolved from technological processes, or the science of technology, which is a way of seeking solutions to tasks or accomplishing tasks. [27]   In its simplest form, a network system allows for the movement of a learning resource, identified in a consultation between a patron and a librarian, from the local elementary school to the public library so the patron can use the resources in the privacy of his own home. The patron may be a thirty-five-year-old seeking information on the United Nations, but this patron may be functioning, mentally, like a nine-year-old elementary school student. The informational unit obtained may be an audiotutorial series of lessons.

The key to the successes wanted for the libraries of tomorrow rests with the people that provide library type services. Libraries, like other complex organizations, reflect the needs of the people served as well as the needs and desires of the people providing the service. Building library service for tomorrow starts with the operators of libraries. In 1965, J. C. R. Licklider speculated that: "In each of three areas, acquisition, organization, and application, we are now greatly limited by the constraint that, whenever information flows into, within, or out of the main store of knowledge, it must pass through people." [28]   And this was perceived as a limitation. If people operating our libraries of today will hamper the full development and operation of libraries of tomorrow we must develop methods to effect change in the staffing of our libraries.

The future holds many surprises for libraries. One thing is certain—the social or service agencies of today are changing and will exist in a different form tomorrow. We can assume that libraries will change with the times. One of the most important changes that will affect libraries is the open school or community school concept. For example, in Wisconsin, the Governor's Commission on Education proposed a number of recommendations that call for the utilization of modern technology as a means for increasing the effectiveness and efficiency of education. Included is the establishment of an educational system that would service all people, from birth to death. It would be meshed with existing programs and it would be a program-generating, program delivery and access agency (or series of agencies in a system) drawing upon business, government, school systems, and libraries for its major resources as it meets needs or desires of the people served. [29]   Suddenly, the library system becomes intertwined with other educational agencies.

A few of the problems that must be addressed and solved in the immediate future are:

1. Duplication of resources between information service units serving the same client group (especially public libraries with children and young adult service units and schools)
2. The multitude of collecting agencies for the nonprint resources, especially the expensive units such as motion pictures
3. Restrictions on access to information in libraries, especially young people trying to use adult sections in libraries and people attempting to access the contents of specialized collections
4. Continued emphasis on print as the prime means for providing information through libraries when so much of the information in our environment is not in the print medium
5. Lack of availability of display equipment for the newer informational storage units
6. Lack of professional role identity of personnel in the library/ information field
7. The lack of long range planning, or futures planning, for libraries as one of the agencies that will continue to operate in the society. + program eval'n.

In the fall of 1971 and spring of 1972, the Ohio State University Center for the Study of Evaluation conducted a three phase, United States Office of Education funded institute for Statewide Library Planning and Evaluation. The existence of this institute for state library agency planners indicated a lack of proficiency in the library field for long range planning and program evaluation. The institute focused on all planning activities, even though the USOE is involved with the states now only as they plan for the use of Library Services and Construction Act funds, following the CIPP (Context, Input, Process, Product) planning-evaluation model frequently referred to in educational planning circles. As a result of this institute, library planners on the state level have been exposed to a learning environment that may have expanded their awareness of not only how to plan for library service, but how to ascertain if the services planned for are indeed being provided.

Planning for libraries must commence. Goals for library service, all types of service as it constitutes a library system, need to be defined. Goal displacement, the process through which means become substituted for claimed goals, must be avoided. [30] Program planning needs to follow the identification of what it is that a library is to do and for whom it will do it. Planning needs to involve the users of libraries as well as library staffs. All states receiving Library Services and Construction Act funds are required to have an operating state advisory council on libraries. These state councils, used correctly, can assist in need identification for goals and programs, as well as in information dissemination concerning library development and operation. Planning councils, broadly based like the state advisory councils, can play a significant role in directing the developmental activity of a local library service unit. As our participatory democracy continues to develop, the people affected by agencies seek involvement in operating that agency. The advisory council provides part of that involvement.

Cooperation between elements in the network, or library system, can help reduce the unnecessary duplication of resources between library types. In addition, as the duplication is reduced, the access to collections will have to increase. These actions must be taken in the light of the goals for library service. Depending on the functions to be performed by the library system, the duplication of materials may be advisable. Cooperation will also facilitate, and be facilitated by, the use of distribution/delivery technologies. The optimum situation between library elements with a network system will make it unimportant where information comes from, just as long as the information is presented to the patron in a usable manner and he is assisted in accomplishing his goals with the use of that information. Cooperation will help to extend resources or to obtain resources. It can also enrich the material and personnel resources available to the patrons served by the library system.

Cooperation can transcend geopolitical boundaries as service networks are established. National networks, consisting of many diverse elements within the library service structure, are possible. The diversity of our national library system may increase the difficulty in developing the cooperative agreements and the defining of the network service systems but it should not reduce the success potential of the total system. That will be true as long as the basic philosophical goal of providing the information to the patron when needed and in a manner usable by that patron is held by all operating elements in the system.

The library of tomorrow—it will be a school/public/academic library functioning as part of the community center. It will use the new technologies of information storage, retrieval, distribution and display, and the technology of instruction. The library of tomorrow will be staffed by a wide range of professionals from fields other than the traditional librarianship or audiovisual technology. The profession of librarianship will radically be changed. In many ways it will take on an appearance of a hybrid profession such as information scientists. The ALA will experience a change in membership—more people from outside the "library school" mold will enter the organization as it addresses itself to the critical issues of library services, library goals. The technicians of the library professions will continue to focus their attention on methods of operating libraries or designing library operating systems to produce a particular service or product. The AECT will become even more involved with the technology of instruction, but its focus will move away from instruction as it exists in the schools. The AECT will further its activity in the library science field through the activities of such divisions as the Information Systems Division.

Inertia will be overcome, and the library elements of today will get together in a system. A network for informational access will be created. Man and the media will have a new relationship.

NOTES

1. Ralph Shaw, "Using Advances in Technology to Make Library Resources More Available," in *Student Use of Libraries: An Inquiry into the Needs of Students, Libraries, and the Educational Process*, Papers of the Conference within a Conference (Chicago: American Library Assn., 1964), p. 73.

2. Herbert Ostrach, "Putting It All Together," *Media and Methods* 4:8 (Jan. 1968).

3. *Ibid.*

4. Henry M. Brickell, *Organizing New York State for Educational Change* (Albany, N.Y.: The University of the State of New York, State Education Dept., 1961), p. 4.

5. Peter F. Drucker, "The Objectives of a Business," in *Reader in Library Administration*, ed. Paul Wasserman and Mary Lee Bundy (Washington, D.C.: Communication Service Corp., 1968), p. 129.

6. Gerald R. Brong, "Paths to Interlibrary Networking for Audiovisual Materials," *Interlibrary Communication and Information Networks*, ed. Joseph Becker (Chicago: American Library Assn., 1971), p. 102.

7. Donald P. Ely, "The Contemporary College Library: Change by Evolution or Revolution," *Educational Technology* 11:17-18 (May 1971).

8. John Vergis, "An Open Forum—Together or Separate," *Audiovisual Instruction* 15:23 (Oct. 1970).

9. John E. Searles, *A System for Instruction* (Scranton, Penn.: International Textbook Co., 1967), p. 22.

10. Bruce R. Joyce, "The Development of Teaching Strategies," *Audiovisual Instruction* 13:820 (Oct. 1968).

11. Hayden R. Smith, "Media Men Arise: What if McLuhan is Right?" *Educational Screen and Audiovisual Guide* 47:19 (June 1968).

12. Robert S. Taylor, "Technology and Libraries," *EDUCOM* 5:5 (May 1970).

13. Nelson N. Foote, "The New Media and Our Total Society," in *The New Media and Education: Their Impact on Society,* ed. Peter H. Rossi and Bruce J. Biddle (Garden City, N.Y.: Doubleday, Anchor Books, 1967), pp. 388-400.

14. Sister Helen Sheehan, "The Library-College Idea: Trend of the Future," *Library Trends* 18:93 (July 1968).

15. Robert M. Gagne, "Educational Technology as Technique," *Educational Technology* 8:11 (15 Nov. 1968).

16. F. Barry Nelson, "Data Transmission in Transition," *Datamation* 17:20-23 (1 Oct. 1971).

17. Brigitte L. Kenney and Frank W. Norwood, "CATV: Visual Library Service," *American Libraries* 2:724 (July-Aug. 1971).

18. H. A. Raymond, "Educational Satellites: Capabilities and Limitations," *Audiovisual Instruction* 17:14 (Jan. 1972).

19. *Ibid.,* p. 15.

20. T. N. Dupuy, *Ferment in College Libraries: The Impact of Information Technology* (Washington, D.C.: Communication Service Corp., 1968), p. 16.

21. Philip M. Morse, *Library Effectiveness: A Systems Approach* (Cambridge, Mass.: Massachusetts Institute of Technology Pr., 1968), p. 1.

22. James S. Martin, "The Audio-Visual Department Comes of Age." *American School and University* 40:24 (Feb. 1968).

23. Smith, p. 19.

24. Gerald R. Brong and Elizabeth F. Pasternak, "The N-I-H-Syndrome," *Library Journal* 95:3877-78 (15 Nov. 1970).

25. Searles, p. 25.

26. Ely, p. 17.

27. Robert Heinich, "Technology and Teacher Productivity," *Audio-Visual Instruction* 16:80 (Jan. 1971).

28. J. C. R. Licklider, *Libraries of the Future* (Cambridge, Mass.: Massachusetts Institute of Technology Pr., 1965), p. 28.

29. Charles A. Wedemeyer and M. Habeed Ghatala, "Wisconsin's Proposed 'Open' School," *Audiovisual Instruction* 17:9-10 (Jan. 1972).

30. John R. Haak, "Goal Determination," *Library Journal* 96:1574 (1 May 1971).

Response | Mr. Heinich

In my comments, I am going to address, to some extent, both Dr. Passow's paper and Mr. Brong's paper. First, I would like to make one comment in regard to an offhand remark that Dr. Passow made at the beginning of his presentation. I hope he didn't mean this exactly as it came out, but the implication was that much of the criticism of the mechanistic (he didn't use the word "mechanistic" but I am using that word) treatment of children in schools could be ascribed to the trend toward hardware delivering information. This story summons up the specter of technology, automatizing the student and so on. I would like to point out that the criticism we have had of the schools, especially of the way students are treated, is almost universally directed toward the way *people* have been treating *people*. We don't need machinery to treat people mechanistically; we are capable of doing it ourselves.

The other side of that coin is the frequently made comment that students resist technology. It's obvious if you watch youth today that they don't resent technology—they use it all the time. What they resent is the technology that we use for our purposes rather than for theirs. In all of their entertainment, they use technology as a base— films, light shows, and so on. Even on the campuses, where students are protesting technology by hitchhiking, it means they are using your technology, not theirs. They gather together at meetings all over the country to protest technology, and I don't think that they get there by walking.

Actually, students use technology as a matter of course. How many of you ever used a picture phone? At San Jose State, when I asked this question of a freshman class, one out of four students had used one. They had all been to Disneyland, of course, and used it there. Those of you who were present at the 1972 AECT convention heard a great presentation of the idea of toys as precursor to technology. Here you have a very interesting example of children using technology as a toy—later it will become a way of life for them.

One time my wife and I were in the home of a Mexican family in Los Angeles. As we were sitting there, the young daughter suddenly burst in. She was about seven or eight years old. It was at Christmastime, and she was carrying one half of a walkie-talkie. As she came into the house she was saying, "Tony, do you read me?" An accent was present, but so was a precision of language. She had great respect for this instrument she was using to communicate with, and she was very conscious that you speak to it in a certain way and that you use certain language. Here is a sophisticated piece of information-handling equipment that has become a part of her life style. I don't think we appreciate the extent to which the young absorb technology and make it a part of the system.

In commenting on Dr. Passow's paper I would say that, in at least a general sense, we definitely are in a trend toward a more variegated pattern in our educational institutions. I think this is observable at both ends of the spectrum. You could almost say that the school system is framed at both ends—at the lower and upper ends—with innovation. At the lower end there is a tremendous emphasis on preschool and nursery school education. With the success of "Sesame Street," of course, and, in the pattern of "Sesame Street," "The Electric Company." After that, the second grade, and tomorrow the world. There is a natural tendency to push upward in a program of this kind. And so we are starting to get a kind of fraying of the institutional structure at the bottom.

At the top, I think the fraying is even more pronounced. For example, in many parts of the country you have three separate kinds of institutions competing for the same adult clientele, including area vocational schools, community colleges with adult education programs, and high schools with adult education programs. I'm not saying that this is good or bad, I am just saying it is happening. We are going to get more and more variegated patterns, particularly in higher education. You see an example in the GED exam, where, for example in Michigan, the age has been lowered to 16 so that a high school dropout can get his equivalency diploma at the same age that his peers are getting it by going through a regular high school. Not only that, but the State Department of Education has a set of cassette tapes that will help him through the program and then, when he passes it, they will pay him for doing so. This allows a separation of some of the students from the regular institutional programs. Colorado is about to do the same thing, and lower their GED age. The high schools, of course, fought it. But it will be lowered to age 16, permitting an alternative choice to students that they don't now have.

The open university concept in England, which is completely predicated on the notion that instruction can be carried on through space and time, and that you don't have to be in direct contact with the student, is another good example. A reflection of this approach in the United States is the Empire State College in New York State.

Pretty soon, if the market is large enough (and it is getting larger), commercial companies will move in and start producing packages that will enable the student to pursue college degrees independently. It has already happened in several ways with several companies. Even within institutions, we are moving more and more toward allowing students to acquire their necessary credits and competencies in ways other than through course attendance. We are increasing the options that students have. In so doing, of course, we increase the likelihood that other institutions can participate in the process.

I could also mention the CLEP program with the Dallas Public

Library and Southern Methodist University, where a student can get an associate in arts degree by taking the test at the Dallas Public Library which develops the reading lists which enable the student to prepare himself for the exams. This type of thing is going to become more prevalent. It is being institutionalized now in a number of places.

The directions in which people will move to take up these new educational options will depend on how the various institutions respond to the possibilities that they now have. But to comment on a remark that was made in one of our discussion groups, to really move away from our present institutional configuration, and the stranglehold of present educational practice, at least two important things have to happen: (1) there needs to be a break in the ways in which we give credit to students and in which we certify them; and (2) we have to set up ways in which the money can follow the student. In other words, the money has to follow the output. Wherever the student output is, that's where money should go. That's not possible now, but we are making some significant breakthroughs in this area, and the breakthroughs are likely to come from outside the system. The Serrano decision can easily do this in California, providing a spur for allowing the money to follow the students. If you do abolish the local property tax as a way of financing public education, the schools can move to funding almost entirely at the state and federal level. The distribution of those funds as state aid can vary considerably, and does not necessarily have to follow the present institutional configuration. Alternate responses can occur much more easily that way.

California has moved in this direction in the community colleges. It permits state aid to junior colleges on the basis of a course under the supervision of, but not necessarily taught by, a certified teacher. This was put in deliberately to cover televised instruction, autotutorial methods, and a number of other techniques where the student is not in direct interface with a teacher, but remains under his general supervision. It would not take much to break that out of its institutional configuration as well, and this could very easily happen. Changes in the ways we allocate state aid may be imminent in the light of certain cases that are pending on performance contracting, and so forth. At the present time we tend to allocate state aid in terms of units of students per so many certified teachers. The way the courts are now ruling on these things, it may go more in terms of output. Certainly the voucher plan allows the money to follow the student. The voucher plan itself, of course, is such a radical departure in the way we allocate money for schooling that practically everybody within the institutions, including school board members, opposes it. But, as you probably know, the first voucher experiment has finally been authorized in California, though on a much more limited basis than had originally been planned.

All of these developments have a tendency to break down our current concept of narrow institutional authority. The technology that we now have available for handling and delivering information will encourage more moves in the direction of breaking down institutional authority. The whole library networking concept will tend to do that also. This is really due to two trends that we have at the present time. One is our capacity to deliver instruction and information no matter where the student is through cabling, satellites, even the U.S. postal service. Whatever the system is, we can deliver instruction and information to the student. The second is the trend toward miniaturization and cartridging. We can allow the student to take information wherever he goes. Those two capabilities are really counter to the kind of institutional framework that we had set up in the past. In a sense, when this happens, when the educational institutions start fraying a little bit, many of us think that some of the pieces will fall into the library as another public institution that could absorb them. But it is also possible that the same forces that are operating to break up the schools could break apart the libraries. If you look at the library only as the territory of the book, it is very possible that, if the appropriate responses aren't made, the library will go back into being an archive, as in the past, and serve simply archival functions. Other institutions will pick up the other kind of work depending on the response that is made, or not made, by libraries.

In this connection, it is difficult to predict the effect of technological innovations on institutions, very difficult. For example, the report on the work of the Commission on the Year 2000 that appeared in *Daedalus* [Summer 1967] noted that when the groups were attempting to predict technological innovations they were exceedingly brilliant, very insightful, and that some very stimulating ideas came forth. But when they started to predict how these things will affect our institutional relationships, all they tended to do was to extend into a larger framework our current relationships. It was very, very difficult to deal with how these institutions might be affected.

Very frequently research doesn't help us out, because researchers often ask questions that are rooted in the wrong context. Qualitative changes frequently come from outside the system, since the research we do tends to operate and accept the within-system paradigm. For example, I'm sure that if we had had educational researchers around at the time of Gutenberg, we would never have gotten the book. They would have investigated whether or not this "thing" printed on this new press could teach as well as, or better than, the illuminated manuscript. Their results would have come out "no significant difference" and they would have said, "Forget it; abandon the whole idea."

It is very difficult to get good answers from educational research-ers because they are not asking the questions that look at what the impact on society would be from an innovation of this kind. To just echo something that Brong said, our new technologies of information handling have the capacity to create new institutional frameworks as well as new industries. We know they will create new industries, but they are likely to create new institutional frameworks as well. I want to mention something that Peter Drucker, widely respected in the management field, says in his book *The Age of Discontinuity.* He calls the knowledge industry one of the four great coming industries of the future. But he also predicts, and this is very interesting when we think in terms of cabling, reprography, and so on, a greater priva-tization of public functions in the future, that a number of the func-tions would be carried on by private companies. For example, if it proves to be profitable, the phone companies, particularly the push button systems, would find it very simple to put in a reference serv-ice for subscribers. This could become a private thing that you could subscribe to, the same way that you subscribe to the Encyclopaedia Britannica Research Program, and Drucker has indicated that it is very likely to go in this direction. We may find new institutional con-figurations, but I don't think we can be complacent about the pivotal role of schools and libraries in relation to the capabilities in informa-tion handling.

If other institutions, such as libraries or private companies, get into the business of helping people directly in terms of instruction and in achieving certain instructional goals and personal learning goals, we are going to need to have some type of evaluation agencies that can give us help in certifying that these packages of instruments, whatever the combination is, do in fact, with certain kinds of popu-lations, produce certain results. We cannot leave this simply to chance. For example, I think we ought to pay very close attention to the efforts of EPIE, the Educational Products Information Ex-change, in its attempt to provide decision-making information to con-sumers in regard to educational products. We may be in that same position ourselves in the near future, needing reliable field data on the performance of instructional instruments, because libraries are going to have to assume some responsibility for the effectiveness of this material, and not simply act as a delivery system, if we really want to gain the confidence of the people we are dealing with.

Lastly, I want to mention one other thing, a very important item, the standardization that Brong referred to in his paper. At present, outside of 16mm films, 35mm slides, and filmstrips, there is very little that is standardized. This may be more of a problem to the li-braries than it is to the public schools. The public school system, as an institution, can be geared to handle nonstandard formats, much as they don't like it. Libraries don't have, and won't be able to have, a lot of the factors that can compensate for nonstandard forms. If we move toward miniaturization, cartridging, and cassettes, you are going to have to rely on the ease of handling, the interchangability of units, and so forth, that come with standardization. So this is a question that I think we are going to have to address ourselves to in the area of technology, and it is not just in the realm of films and tapes, but also in the compatability of information systems, of computer programs and computer-assisted instruction systems which now need translators from one system to the other. We are going to have to attend to this problem in the future.

Past and Present Efforts at Coordination of Library Services at the Community Level

Presentation:
KATHLEEN MOLZ

Response:
MILDRED FRARY

The lending of books and the provision of general reference services to the local community have been, historically, the unique prerogatives of the free public library. Unlike academic or school libraries, which were initially developed to serve the needs of their respective clienteles of students and faculties, the public library began as an agency of self-education, primarily for adults. Its relationship with the public school movement was somewhat ambivalent. On the one hand, some nineteenth-century partisans of the public library regarded the newly formed institution as the "crowning glory" of the public school system intended to correct "an existing defect in our otherwise admirable system of public education." [1] Conversely, other equally vocal proponents of the public library argued that it would serve as an alternative to formal education affording the general public opportunities to learn through "an independent educational agency coordinate with, rather than subsidiary to, the public school." [2] This latter view is reflected in Dickens's novel *Hard Times*, where the horrors of the fact-ridden curriculum of Mr. Gradgrind's day school are contrasted with the appeal of Coketown's public library to its hard-working residents.

With the diminution of school district public libraries and the gradual increase of free town libraries, the public library sought to chart its course through the uncertain mazes of American educa-

Kathleen Molz is Chief, Planning Staff, Bureau of Libraries and Educational Technology, U.S. Office of Education, Washington, D.C.

Mildred Frary is the Director, Library Services, Los Angeles City Unified School District, Los Angeles, California.

tional policy as an independent instrument for the instruction of
the public. It was referred to as a "people's university," where there
were no criteria for admission, no curricular standards, and, perhaps equally significant, no certification upon completion of the
learning task. Graduates of the "people's university" might indeed
be better educated, but, unfortunately, they had no cluster of letters
after their names to put on the forms they filled out for prospective employers.

If the hard-fought battle for independence of the public schools
was won by the public library, then the victory was indeed Pyrrhic.
As matters stand now, $.40 of every tax dollar expended by local and
state governments for all services finds its way into the support of
the public schools; the figure for public library support is $.0053.
Hard-pressed public librarians can only find the answers to this
paucity of support in the pages of history: First, the public library,
in stressing its benefits to those machinists, engineers, and instrument makers originally identified as its proper clients, could not have
anticipated the impact of Federal aid to higher education which,
through the Morrill Land Grant Act of 1862 and numerous provisions
since that date, ultimately made possible postsecondary education
for countless Americans. Second, the public library's founders had
no way of predicting the availability of inexpensive reading materials
made possible by the paperback book industry. And last, no one, not
even the founders of the common school movement, could have fore-
seen the impact on educational theory of John Dewey. As Lawrence
A. Cremin has pointed out, American education was initially marked
by diversity: the public libraries and lyceums, the mechanics' insti-
tutes and agricultural societies, the penny newspapers and dime
novels. Cognizant of this variety, Dewey nonetheless asserted the
complaint that industrialism was destroying the educational functions carried on by home, shop, neighborhood, and church. In what
Cremin terms "the grand jeté of twentieth-century educational
theory," Dewey identified the public school as "society's great instrument for shaping its own destiny." [3]

The centricity of the public school in public education became so
well established that the schools added to their traditional tuitional
concerns for children an entire gamut of societal responsibilities,
ranging from health and nutritional care to driver instruction and
sex education. Before this obtrusive agency, the public library inevitably lost any major pretensions to serving as the "crowning
glory" of the public school system, or even to affording an alternative
to it. Instead, the public library, especially during the period of the
student-use crisis, well-identified during the early and mid-sixties,
found itself increasingly drawn toward the vortex of formal school-

ing, its resources deployed for student homework, college term papers, and correspondence lessons. [4]

If any year were to be acknowledged as the turning point in the modern course of the public library, then 1965 would seem an appropriate choice. For the first time, the nation's town and metropolitan libraries became eligible for benefits under the federally supported Library Services and Construction Act, which had been a program of support solely to rural areas until the 1964 amendments. Then too, with the promise of Federal funds for construction, long-range building programs were instituted to provide much needed facilities for students in search of materials for their ubiquitous term papers.

Yet, the year also signalized the passage of two other major pieces of Federal library legislation supporting, for the first time, the libraries of academic institutions (Higher Education Act of 1965, Title II-A) and those of the public schools (Elementary and Secondary Education Act, Title II). The growth of libraries, especially those in community and junior colleges, as well as the heightened activity of children's services within the public schools, have undeniably affected the role of the public library, an effect which will be discussed later in this paper.

Viewed in retrospect, 1965 may well have been the crest of the wave. Having shown a 32 percent increase in the number of patron transactions during the first five years of the 1960s, public libraries in the larger American communities (those having over 100,000 inhabitants) showed a 16 percent decline in circulation from 1965 to 1968, the last year for which nationally aggregated data are available. [5] Communities of this size embrace many of the nation's outstanding public library systems, such as those of Cleveland, Baltimore, and Detroit, all of which fell heir during these years to the problems of shifting populations and inner-city decay.

At the same time as many of the nation's larger public libraries were witnessing a decline in patron transactions, experimentation was begun with neighborhood-based "outreach" projects in response to the educational plight of the functionally illiterate adults and undereducated children who constituted their new constituents. For the most part, these "outreach" projects fell outside the mainstream of traditional public library service. Rented storefront facilities often proved more hospitable to rap sessions, paperback books, audiovisual materials, and indigenous publishing programs than the Carnegie branch with its central charging desk, rows of bookstacks, and Dewey classification schemes. Although some proved successful and others failed, these innovative programs, affording informational and educational services to the poor, served as harbingers of the shift in public libraries from a supplier-based orientation to a user-based one.

Public librarians entered the decade of the seventies uneasily. Escalating costs, tight money constraints, reductions of staff through government-imposed freezes, and dwindling circulation statistics were hardly an augury of future growth. Small wonder that the Public Library Association of the American Library Association published its first major report of the decade under the title *A Strategy for Public Library Change.* While calling for an "eloquent statement to direct widespread attention to the American public library as an active community agent capable of meeting the real needs of real people today and in the future," [6] the report nonetheless detailed some of the critical problems facing the providers of community library service, among them failure to communicate, rigidity in management, fiscal insignificance, lack of defined objectives, and inability to measure performance.

Underlying all of these is the recognition, whether spoken or unspoken by public librarians, that the work they are performing may no longer have significant relevance to the public they ostensibly serve. Within the context of its nineteenth-century founding, the public library afforded the following three major services: (1) through its provisions of current newspapers and periodicals, the library was a fount of public information; (2) through its retrospective collections of past writers of eminence, it served as the purveyor of the cultural and historical record; and (3) through its circulation of books to the ordinary household, it became the chief instrumentality for the free distribution of books in a democratic society. All of these functions were inextricably linked with the primacy of the printed word as a medium of communication and, more to the point, the printed word within what was then the relatively expensive confines of the book.

Both technological advancements and societal changes have affected these service functions: (1) radio and television are now the prime sources of public information; (2) editions of Shakespeare and Jane Austen are available in the paperback racks of many local and all college bookstores; and (3) the book club and the discount store are making serious inroads into the library's claim as the unique disseminator of books. In light of the diversity of educational films, filmstrips, and broadcasts now available to American students, even the book itself is being challenged as a major tool of education.

In addition to these social changes, public librarians were also compelled to reckon with the advent of a major school library movement and the development of new community and junior college libraries. Since 1965, aided by the ESEA II program, a total of 23,932 public schools have established school media centers, and an additional 60,121 schools have made improvements. The proportion of public schools with media centers has increased from 52 to 85 percent, the elementary schools being the primary beneficiaries since many secondary schools had media centers prior to the passage of ESEA. The proliferation of junior and community colleges, with their attendant requirements for student libraries, is also indicative of a new dimension for library usage and service. In the fall of 1969, ninety-nine totally new academic institutions (seventy-eight of which were two-year institutions) were reported as having been established during the preceding year, and each of these contributed a new library to the growing universe of academic libraries.

Although many school and campus libraries still fall short of the requirements cited in professional standards, the fact remains that a sizeable portion of the American public is being afforded different options to obtain materials for their educational and cultural advancement than those previously dispensed by the downtown public library and its neighborhood branches. However much the distinctions among types of libraries may be honored by professional librarians, these do not deter the user from gravitating to the facility that proves itself most accessible or more responsive to his needs.

The blurring of type-of-library turfs is amply borne out by the study of student use of libraries conducted by the Philadelphia Student Library Research Center. Among the older children (those in grades six to twelve) 42 percent were shown to have used *both school and public libraries;* 13 percent used *only the public library;* 32 percent used *only the school library;* and 13 percent found *other sources,* such as home libraries or bookstores, to furnish their materials. [7] Latent in any analysis of multifacility use is, of course, the nagging proposition that such usage is needlessly duplicative. Hence, the 1970 *Report of the Commissioner of Education's Committee on Library Development,* which recommended the cessation of services for young children in the public libraries of New York State and the transfer of these services to school libraries, stressed as its first postulate: "To avoid unnecessary duplication." [8]

Regardless of the developments to institute libraries in terms of special clienteles, a persistent leit motif has been sounded within the framework of professional librarianship calling for interlibrary cooperation and coordination. Surely it is no accident that toward the close of the last century the National Education Association afforded a home to a library department, or that the 1936 Statute, establishing a unit for library services within the U.S. Office of Education, should have enunciated as part of its mission "fostering coordination of public and school library service," and again, "fostering Nation-wide coordination of research material among the more scholarly libraries. ..." [9]

Within broad terms, all Federal legislation in support of libraries of any type stresses the need for libraries to work together cooperatively in pursuit of common aims. The Library Services and Construction Act, Title III, "Interlibrary Cooperation," funds only those projects which assure the effective coordination of the resources of multitype libraries; under the Special Purpose Grants provision of Title II-A of the Higher Education Act, "joint-use facilities" are specified for eligible funds; and the Elementary and Secondary Education Act, Title II, mandates assurance that there be coordination at both State and local levels with respect to the program carried out under the public library authority.

Although no one has yet attempted a complete morphology of all the varieties of interlibrary cooperation, the majority of the activity is primarily centered around three areas: (1) bibliography, (2) technical processing, and (3) reference. The compilation of union lists of serials or microforms is an example of the first; the cataloging of books and materials for an aggregate of libraries by some central agency typifies the second; and the third is exemplified by the interlibrary loan and reference network, founded on a principle of hierarchial support by means of which the user's request is handled by a succession of increasingly sophisticated agencies until the document is located or the answer found.

All of these activities have certain common goals: better public service; economy; the reduction of duplicative work; efficiency; and speed. Yet, however meritorious such goals are, they are primarily determined by professional librarians, and may not necessarily represent those which the public itself would enunciate.

Put another way, the activities common to interlibrary cooperation or interinstitutional coordination assume on the part of the user some degree of educational perspicacity, some sense that out of the bibliographical maze his needs for knowledge can be met. Yet, many people can neither perceive nor articulate their knowledge needs, one reason, perhaps, why libraries have seemed so often irrelevant to the poor.

Counter to the more traditional interinstitutional approach, which depends for its success on communality of bibliographical entry or uniformity of filing rules, has been a movement of direct involvement with the community itself, an involvement that is based not only on an assessment of the knowledge needs of the community, but also on the participation of the community in determining its requirements and establishing policy to direct its own educational program. Under these terms, "community" library service is not predicated on a span of control leading from the smallest agency to the next largest, and so on, but is instead directed toward a specific neighborhood where a center for learning is formed, stressing services and programs rather than books, conferring insight rather than mere information, and affording values rather than facts. These learning centers, which crop up under various names, such as community learning center, library learning center, or neighborhood learning center, deemphasize processing of materials or their classification. Indeed, they go further in eliminating circulation procedures, often requiring no formal registration and assessing no charges for overdue returns.

It has been observed that some of the great advances in surgery and medicine were undeniable results of major wars, when the restoration of fighting men to the front proved itself a national priority, not a compassionate necessity. Certainly, the war on poverty has enjoined comparable results in energizing the public service agencies toward probing more deeply into the causes and effects of poverty, whether it be educational or economic, or indeed both. Both libraries and schools have benefited from these probes. At a time when institutional change is being called for, the community learning center provides a very special environment responsive to and inspired by a specific neighborhood.

What is a community learning center? Lowell A. Martin, a nationally known consultant to one such center, Philadelphia's Action Library, has defined its components in this way:

(1) a community-based project, which is free of the traditional restrictions of established schools and libraries,

(2) a community-oriented program which involves students and other persons from the neighborhood in most aspects of its operation, including staffing,

(3) provision of multimedia resources selected to interest children and young people,

(4) a multistaff mix, including service teams of librarians, teachers, and other specialists,

(5) involvement of parents in the learning process, as well as children and young people,

(6) activities designed to attract [and] stimulate young people and to develop their interests (rather than simply to be available for those with the initiative to seek out the center),

(7) interagency sponsorship by the school systems and the public library, with the overall goal of fostering change in these library systems. [10]

Now operational in a low-income community in Philadelphia's south-central area, the Action Library fully demonstrates these concepts. Formed through a coalition of the city's entire educational system, including the public, diocesan, and private schools and the public library, the Action Library is also responsive to a Community Advisory Board, which serves as the interpreter of the community to the staff of the learning center. The staff is composed of librarians, AV specialists, and reading teachers drawn from both the schools and the public library system, as well as paraprofessionals recruited from the community itself. Audiovisual equipment, including recordings, closed-circuit television, and film, cohabits quite gently with the paperback books on display. And, although no space is ever out of bounds within the center to anyone, an alcove furnished in the style of an ordinary living room provides sanctuary to the adults in search of a quiet place to watch TV or read a popular magazine.

The Philadelphia learning center is not designed nor intended to replace the traditional school or public library, since school assignments and research inquiries will still be the responsibility of these latter agencies. The center, then, should not be viewed in a competitive sense, as a substitute for existing institutions, but rather as an agency within its own right having unique capacities to influence the educational growth of the community it serves.

Philadelphia's Action Library, although more thoroughly researched and evaluated than any other library-based learning center, is by no means unique. The Langston Hughes Community Library and Cultural Center, begun in 1969, serves a black community in the borough of Queens, New York. Advised by its own Board of Directors, the Center not only features black heritage materials, it also affords opportunities for school-sponsored tutorial programs directed by the New York Board of Education. In New Mexico, the Albuquerque Model Cities Library stresses programs and materials of particular relevance to its Chicano community, comprising such areas of interest as the American Southwest, the American Indian, and the Spanish-speaking American. Educational toys as well as books are freely circulated, and the participants in the program can request a personal film showing as well as watch their favorite TV shows. Rochester, New York, houses the Phillis Wheatley Community Library, a black-oriented community learning center featuring individual study carrels that enable its patron to view a film or hear a tape without distraction to others.

Not yet operational but in the planning stage are other centers designed with the community learning concept in mind. Olney, a small Texas town with only 4,000 inhabitants, intends to merge its public and school libraries into a unified cultural center, embracing the informational and educational needs of a total community from preschool child to the aging. Nor is the community college exempt from this activity: the library of St. Louis's Florissant Valley Community College proposes to serve as the center of an experimental project involving a number of community organizations which promote opportunities for learning and education. Participants engaged in learning activities, whether these be attendance at an arts course sponsored by a local museum or a black studies program held at a local public library, could conceivably earn college credits for their noncampus-based work.

The variables attendant upon the development of a community learning center are many; certainly each one, as it is planned and instituted, must prove itself responsive to the community it serves. Yet, all the centers are alike in one respect, namely, their provision of an alternative to, not a displacement of, the educational structure as it now stands. The need for our technical processing centers and reference networks will not be negated by the informal educational strategies of the learning center, which makes no pretension to bibliographical expertise or totality of resources. Yet, some will still view the center as a threat to established institutions of learning. Others, however, will concede that in an intensively pluralistic society, replete with many and very diverse means of communication, no one agency can hold the sole claim to the mine of knowledge. As James S. Coleman observes: "Schools as they now exist were designed for an information-poor society, in part to give a child vicarious experience through books and contact with a teacher. Obviously that function is altered radically by television, radio, and other media outside the school." [11] His comments would be equally true of traditional libraries, which find themselves in an informationally affluent culture often bypassed by the very people they most desire to serve.

It is not without significance that the *Congressional Record* of July 23, 1971, should reprint verbatim the contents of the July 1971 issue of *Prometheus*, the bulletin of the Archives of Institutional Change, as follows:

> We recommend the establishment of a new type of community learning center, a center that would marshal the services and make available the cultural (including those of the barrio and ghetto), educational, and business and industry resources of the total community. The community learning centers would help any learner obtain the kind of relevant education that is required by the learner at that time. We conceive of these community learning centers providing education for the world of work, continuing academic studies or for personal development and fulfillment. [12]

Even though the promise of these concepts is already being fulfilled, as public, school, and academic libraries yield to a new function, there is some satisfaction in noting that the idea of a community learning center is being verbalized in a journal deriving its title from the name of the Greek titan who stole fire from heaven as a gift for man.

NOTES

1. For an excellent description of the ideologies attendant on the foundation of the American public library see the 1852 "Report on the Trustees of the Public Library of the City of Boston," reproduced in full as Appendix V in Jesse H. Shera, *Foundations of the American Public Library* (New Haven, Conn.: Shoe String, 1965), pp. 267-90, *passim*.

2. Sidney Ditzion, *Arsenals of a Democratic Culture* (Chicago: American Library Assn., 1947), p. 85.

3. Lawrence A. Cremin, *The Genius of American Education* (New York: Vintage Books, 1965), pp. 8-9.

4. In June of 1963, the American Library Association sponsored a Conference within a Conference devoted to the "needs of students, libraries, and the educational process." Proceedings of the conference were published by the American Library Association, *Student Use of Libraries* (Chicago: American Library Assn., 1964), 212 p. *passim*.

5. Statistics for public library usage are derived from the following:

USOE Library Services Branch, *Statistics of Public Library Systems Serving Populations of 100,000 or More: Fiscal Year 1960* (Washington, D.C.: GPO, Nov. 1961), OE 15033, 24 pp.

USOE National Center for Educational Statistics, *Statistics of Public Libraries Serving Communities With at Least 25,000 Inhabitants: 1965* (Washington, D.C.: GPO, 1968), OE 15068, 65 pp.

USOE National Center for Educational Statistics, *Statistics of Public Libraries Serving Areas With at Least 25,000 Inhabitants: 1968* (Washington, D.C.: GPO, 1970), OE 15068, 144 pp.

6. Allie Beth Martin, *A Strategy for Public Library Change* (Chicago: American Library Assn., 1972), p. 50.

7. John Q. Benford, "The Philadelphia Project," *Library Journal* (15 June 1971), p. 2044.

8. New York State Education Dept. *Report of the Commissioner of Education's Committee on Library Development* (Albany, N.Y.: The Department, 1970), p. 27.

9. Douglas M. Knight and E. Shepley Nourse, eds., *Libraries at Large* (New York and London: Bowker, 1969), p. 468.

10. Lowell A. Martin, "The Philadelphia Project: The Action Library, Its Purpose and Program," photo-offset (Philadelphia: Philadelphia Student Library Project, 1 Dec. 1971), p. 1.

11. James S. Coleman, "Forget About Learning in School," *The [Baltimore] Sun*, 12 Mar. 1972, p. K 1.

12. "Archives of Institutional Change," *Congressional Record-Senate* (23 July 1971), S 11939.

Response | Ms. Frary

My reactions to Miss Molz's paper center on two themes—definitions and impediments—and they are addressed not to past efforts at coordination of library services, but to present and future efforts. The paper is a brilliant and literate statement about the uneasy relationship of public and school libraries in the past, and it presents tantalizing glimpses of some demonstration projects that may help us change this relationship in the future.

DEFINITIONS

Throughout this conference I have been troubled by terminology and by the different meanings that persons from different backgrounds are attaching to some common words—students, service, community, coordination. Each of you knows what he is talking about, I'm sure, and I know a little bit about what I think you are talking about.

What is a community? The paper makes reference to large "communities" such as Cleveland, Baltimore, Philadelphia, Detroit, and it also makes reference to neighborhood communities, to special clientele communities, to a community such as Olney, Texas, with its 4,000 inhabitants. When I hear this, I think "How wonderful it would be to have a total community of only 4,000 people to work with!" My high schools in Los Angeles have about that many students each.

Being a librarian, and in large part a children's librarian, I naturally turned to a simple dictionary for a definition. The simplest definition calls a community "a number of people having common ties or interests living in the same place and subject to the same laws." Community obviously has many more meanings than this, and we need to develop precision in what we say. The concept of total community library service is capable of an infinite variety of meanings.

What is library service? The papers at this conference suggest that providing material for educational and cultural advancement is library service, that responding to the needs of the community is service, that instruction is service, and that learning should be a measurable result of service. The dictionary defines service as "helpful activity, the supplying of articles, commodities, activities, required or demanded." Library service can be many things but we all know that there must be some output measurement, some way of knowing that people have been helped. This is where PPBS comes into the picture.

What is coordination? Is it not an interinstitutional approach to a common problem? The dictionary calls coordination "harmonious adjustment for working together." One could put all of these definitions together and say that total community library service means a number of institutions, in harmonious adjustment, supplying helpful activities involving educational resources and related services demanded or requested by a group of people having common ties or interests and living in the same place.

This doesn't sound like much of a working definition. Is this what we mean? If not, what do we mean? What is our overall goal? Do we really have coordinated community library service as our goal, or are we being pressured into this by factors outside our control? The budget makers see duplication and waste in our present organization for library service. On the other hand, users, unlike professional librarians, fail to see the fine distinctions we have drawn between public, school, special, and academic library service. These fine distinctions have not kept users from gravitating to the facility that proves most accessible and most responsive to their needs. If there is duplication and waste, and if users don't care about our distinctions, what prevents us from moving to a unified resource center approach embracing all the informational and educational needs of a community?

Do we really have a goal for coordinated service, or is this something we are being scared into? Do we really believe that every human being living in the United States has a right to reasonable access to any information and to all published and otherwise produced material that he needs for whatever purpose is important to him? Is that our goal? If it is not, what is it? Do we have clear objectives?

In the account of past and present efforts I noticed a few recurring objectives for cooperation—to provide better service, to achieve economy, to reduce duplication, to promote efficiency, to speed up service. All of these objectives seem more product-oriented than user-oriented. The most important recurring objective was

to satisfy expressed learning needs of the community. How coordination can be effective toward achieving these desired objectives
is not really clear. The paper reminds us strongly that federal legislation encourages and even mandates cooperation. I would guess,
and I believe it to be true, that most of the demonstration projects
which have been mentioned here were funded with something other
than local tax money. How else does one allow for the necessary
research, the capital outlay, the evaluation? Coordination on a large
scale requires something more in effort and in staff than can be
accomplished by regular workers on regular budgets. Such money
is hard to get from local sources.

SOME IMPEDIMENTS AND PROBLEMS

My second major concern is with impediments to change—the
physical, political, fiscal, legal, psychological. If we have been unable, through our present structure for library service, to achieve
coordination, if we can't improve or change what we now have, what
makes us think we can expiate past sins by creating a new structure,
which would soon fall victim itself to the same kind of impediments?

Inherent in the approach of some of the demonstration projects
mentioned here—for instance, the Action Library and the Olney,
Texas, project—is an effort to escape from the negative image that
libraries have built for themselves and from the burden of past
failures at coordination of resources and services. A new broom
sweeps clean. An Action Library can succeed where all else has
failed. Many examples of this desire to escape from the failures of
the past have come up in our group discussions.

Some examples come from my own experience. We had fairly
good cooperation between public and school libraries in Los Angeles
before the great student influx in the late '50s and '60s. We had
plenty of advance warning that a student wave would crest, and we
worked hard to build up both school and public libraries. The libraries were too small, of course; there was never enough money to
do it right. The public library made some bad decisions on location,
building as part of other community services such as police and fire
stations. Economical, yes, but locations which later turned off a
lot of kids. We both went our merry ways, cooperating by accident.
The school libraries were open early, the public libraries were open
late. We lived through the era of maximum student use of libraries
and of spill-over to the public library. Today we are in a different
era, one in which many students dislike the institution of the school,
and of the public library, associating both with repression, and

lacking the motivation to make use of library resources. Getting over this problem will not be easy, but I seriously wonder if creating a new alternative institution is the answer.

Even those librarians who are optimistic about the future, and eager to make changes, are hampered by lack of information on what is going on and what is working well. Finding out from the literature is a frustrating experience, and we don't all have the benefit of attending conferences like this one where we can have face-to-face contact with many of those who are doing the new things. With so many interesting projects exploring alternative arrangements for library service going on right now, it is a shame that it is so difficult to find out the results and benefit by their experience. Since "student" and "community" mean so many different things, I know that I can't transfer all of the findings of the Philadelphia student library use project back to Los Angeles, but I do feel that I have a right to get at the research findings and make up my own mind about what elements can work in our city. I'm pretty sure that some of the data about student use of libraries will be just as relevant to Watts, or even to Beverly Hills, as it is to Philadelphia.

The Action Library and the Olney project are too new to have produced much yet of an evaluative nature, but we will want to know in time what did and did not work. There are many ways to evaluate, and some of these I am suspicious of. For one thing, if you are expecting to get more money from Federal sources, you pretty nearly have to tell them that you are succeeding in meeting your objectives, whether you are or not. Evaluators look for impact indicators and laugh at such primitive measures as circulation statistics. As has been pointed out many times in this conference, we need to work very hard on developing new ways to measure services.

From Kathleen Molz's discussion on past and present efforts at coordination of library services we can infer some other constraints. For one thing, we live in real fear of the charge of duplication of effort and waste of public money. Part of this fear is the realization that any realignment of services, of school and public library service, for instance, might result in the elimination of jobs, the reclassification to lower salary levels, of sweeping changes in the scope of our day-to-day work. Our fear is a very human fear. The New York State proposal that library service to school-aged children be placed in the school library and eliminated from the public library ran exactly up against these fears. The idea is certainly not new and the response is certainly predictable.

There are other constraints that are just as serious, though sometimes easy for experts to brush aside—the financial constraints. In Los Angeles we can't support existing library service, let alone improve it. Finding money to experiment with alternatives to present service is not as easy as Dr. Trump implies. We don't have the money and we don't know where it can come from. The idea of creating a new kind of library needs to be seen in the context of what we are now able to do. In Los Angeles, for instance, the Garfield High School Library seats forty-three students. There are 3,000 students in that school. There is no other space unless we eliminate physical education and take over the gym. Not likely, since physical education is very important to these young people. The public library branches available to this neighborhood are just as deficient in space and resources. Cooperation between school libraries and public libraries moves at a slow pace, partly because of the resistance of Boards of Trustees. These Boards, after a fashion, represent the community, but they tend to be extremely conservative. The residents of the community have even rioted for a library, but still there isn't money for one, because bond issues don't pass. Here is a real dilemma, one that involves only one school, but is indicative of the scale of the problem.

The political aspects of trying to restructure library service bother me. We live in a political society. It is no secret that there are plenty of federal administrators and program officers who are looking for innovative projects that match current guidelines and priorities. After the Philadelphia project, that kind of approach will no longer be innovative. We may copy it, but we can't get Federal money to do so. The impact of Federal legislation and Federal programs on changes in both school and public libraries can't be overstated. Most of the changes that have come about in recent years have been the result of Federal funding. Unfortunately, as administrations change, priorities often die and new ones are substituted. There are very real problems associated with the situation where projects turn on and turn off at the whim of changing administrations.

There are also many protective and impeding laws that have varying effects on coordination of services. These laws may involve such things as certification of personnel, rigid building codes, prescribed curricula. A school building may fall down in an earthquake in Los Angeles, but you can not put the children in a storefront library and continue their education because the storefront is not approved for safety by the State Department of Education.

The physical facilities in which we operate frequently impede service. The schools in some parts of Los Angeles are beginning to look more like prisons than schools. The vandalism cost is $2 million a year. Once you get inside the gate in the morning, you are locked in for the rest of the day. What do you do for the questing mind in an environment like that? How do you make use of the community as a learning environment if the students are locked in for the day?

In conclusion, I think that we see from this paper and from others at the conference that coordination is feasible and is happening in many aspects of library service, especially the technical and bibliographical. In order to answer the questions of how school and public libraries might better be coordinated, there are some exploratory projects underway. New approaches to service have been proposed. The real answer to combining the concept of the learning resource center of the school with the traditional freedom of access and self-directed learning opportunity of the public library has yet to be resolved. Missing from the paper, perhaps, are many small examples of coordination, straws in the wind, that have arisen spontaneously and are terribly important at the grass roots level. Missing also from the paper is much information on the ways in which special and academic libraries can best be coordinated into a total service pattern. Also missing is evidence of much concern for adults, especially for older adults. We should be planning now for the time when the students who created the great public library crisis of the '60s reach senior citizen status. When they reach that stage, will we have removed the barriers that we erected in the '60s to prevent their taking all the space? They will still remember, although most of us may not be around to see it. They will also be voting for or against libraries at that time. Senior citizens are not very likely, in most cases, to vote for things that benefit only the young.

Issues
and
Recommendations

SUMMARIES OF DISCUSSIONS

Conferees were assigned to one of four discussion groups, and stayed with this group for discussions following the presentation and critique of each of the four commissioned background papers. At the final session of the conference, two representatives from each discussion group made short reports to the entire conference group on what they saw as the major issues arising from the papers and the discussions.

Kenneth Carruthers (discussion group 1)

Professionally, I am an architect, affiliated with a city planning firm. This gives me an opportunity to look at library matters as a layman or an outsider. I was prepared to come to the conference and argue that libraries as pieces of architecture, and libraries as institutions, are totally irrelevant to much of the community. I am still willing to reach that conclusion, but some very large steps would have to be taken to reach that conclusion, that I now think none of us is prepared to take.

I relate my remarks chiefly to three points I have noted down at this conference. The first point which really caught my interest was Mr. Coletta's paper about the management issues involved in measuring library services and establishing accountability. The second point was that there is obviously an increasing awareness, although

I don't believe a complete acceptance, of the impact of technology on library services. I don't think any of us are really able to measure the full extent of the revolution in communications media that we are immersed in. The third point that caught my attention was the pilot project in Philadelphia, the Action Library, where all sorts of new techniques, with broad institutional and community participation, are in use to try out a new kind of library service pattern in one city.

The first point, the management and accountability aspect, and the third point, the pilot project, reflect, I believe, the emergence of a rational, if intuitive, planning process in libraries, which I believe needs to be stressed further. If planners can be of assistance to you, it would be in this area. As professional planners, we have developed effective methodologies for looking at and treating the conditions of human settlement. We are looking at human settlements in their broadest context. Libraries and library services, in this view, are part of the process. I believe that you cannot study library problems, or the library delivery system, out of the context of the total community picture today. I realize that it is only through comprehensive studies that one would really be able to know the status of libraries today. You are all aware of your problems, but until you analyze them systematically and rationally, you feel unable to proceed. Perhaps planners can help. Our approach is an interdisciplinary one, looking at all of the economic, social, political, and technological aspects of the city. You have to look at library services in the same interdisciplinary fashion.

Planning has two phases, first you analyze and then you synthesize. In the analytical stage comes the tracing of past trends. This is done statistically if possible, and I believe that there are reasonably good statistics available for library services. While we can't always quantify the cultural aspects that we are dealing with, we can make reasonable judgments on their impact. There are ways of gauging quality just as there are ways of adding up quantity. If you can trace past trends in library delivery systems, you should be able to determine realistically where you are today and to project these trends accurately into the future, assuming you don't make any changes in the system. But not until you really have this all laid out in front of you are you able to make judgments on where you want to go.

The final step is to institute action programs which will enable you to reach these goals. As in any good planning process, there must be ways of evaluating and changing as you move along on these programs, because your objectives will change and your goals will change. We have been talking at this conference about instituting change and finding some rational methodology to accomplish change. I want to emphasize that constructive change can come about only after you know where you are today. Although there appears to have been a great deal of research done on library service problems, I don't believe it has all been brought together in usable form, and I don't believe there exists a real methodology whereby you can rationally collect and graphically portray the situation. As I said, we have developed such methodologies in urban planning and I believe that others can be devised for looking at library delivery systems on the national, regional, community, or neighborhood scale.

I don't know if I have fairly expressed all the judgments of my group but we did arrive at one conclusion. Our specific suggestion was this, that prototype research projects should be sponsored by NEA and ALA jointly which would attempt to look at the question of total community library service empirically. These should involve multidisciplinary research teams, consisting of librarians, educators, sociologists, and planners, both economic and urban. We think that only in this way, through pilot projects in specified communities, can we get at the root of the problem. Already, several pilot projects sponsored by the U.S. Office of Education are underway in various parts of the country. We would like to suggest that others, under different sponsorship and in different circumstances, would be most valuable.

Augusta Baker (discussion group 1)

It is impossible for me to convey to you any real sense of the wide range of thinking and discussion which went on in group 1. I think I can safely say that our group will leave this conference with many ideas for action and a desire to share these ideas with others and to get things moving in our own backyards. As we formulated our recommendations, we became increasingly aware that we were not being especially innovative, that many of these things had been said before, but that perhaps the time had come when they should be translated into action.

When we came to a discussion of Dr. Passow's paper and Dr. Trump's critique, we were especially taken with Dr. Trump's proposal for a coordinator of community learning resources. Our group felt that each community must determine who initiates such coordination. It could come from interested lay personnel, but it will probably come from persons in established libraries and schools. In many communities the public library may take the initiative since it is already responsible to the broadest public. We feel that this concept should be developed and tested. A board of this type should take the initiative for bringing together the various parts of the community for affirmative, professional, interdisciplinary planning of alternatives for total community information services. This planning must involve an assessment of the present situation, a consideration of trends in library services, and the formulation of specific goals. The output of such planning should be specific action programs tailored to the needs of individual communities. We urge that funding for planning studies of this kind be recognized as legitimate activities for support under such things as the Library Services and Construction Act.

Mr. Coletta's paper and Mr. Swartz's critique brought about some division of opinion in our group. Some members felt that tools of management such as PPBS can and should be applied to libraries, while others strongly questioned their applicability. The group felt, however, that since governmental authorities at all levels are increasingly demanding accountability and evaluation, libraries must take steps to see that these things are done properly. It is one thing for us to say that certain parts of library service can't be quantified, but we get nowhere by dragging our heels. Therefore we recommend that some well-planned studies be undertaken to develop ways of measuring library services and of specifying library objectives and goals. Deliberate efforts are needed in the development of methodologies for measuring program impact. We should borrow what we can, and develop what we must.

In all our discussions we felt that we needed a clearer definition of some of the terminology used. We found ourselves using the phrase "total community library service" in many ways. A project aimed specifically at gathering descriptive data on what is actually occurring today in the coordination of library services within the community would be valuable. Also valuable would be some thoughtful analysis of the concept of total community library service—articles and perhaps further regional conferences.

A study is also needed to determine the kind of educational preparation necessary to prepare personnel for total community library responsibilities. We know of no efforts even to explore the implications this concept has for the training of future teachers and librarians. In our discussion of the kinds of changes that would be necessary in the staffing patterns for community information centers, especially those which would go beyond the present role of the library, we felt a great lack of information. One possibility might be joint membership for such staff members in related professional organizations such as ALA and NEA.

One of our specific suggestions is that a feasibility study is needed to show the possibility of operating an around-the-clock network of information service through the coordination of existing community library resources.

We also feel strongly that the federal government should take more of the responsibility for the collection, the evaluation, and the dissemination of the results of federally funded projects in education and library services. These reports, although they are in the public domain, are rarely in a form usable by the practicing professional. ERIC is all right, perhaps, for the scholar on the campus, but it isn't too helpful to the firing-line professional. Such reports should include some account of problems as well as failures.

Ralph Conant (discussion group 2)

The basic issue facing this conference, and underlying all our group discussions, was the question of how public and other library services at the community level can best be coordinated with the public education system in efforts to try out new approaches to the delivery of services. Mr. Coletta covered some new directions in the delivery of municipal services and told us how these new directions might affect libraries and educational institutions. What his contribution actually amounted to was the presentation of some management tools which are available for planning and measuring the kinds of services we render. He presented his case very well. Mr. Swartz, however, pointed out quite appropriately that such a tool as PPBS might also be used to further rigidify our school and library systems at the very point when they need flexibility for better coordination with other agencies. In our group discussion we were fortunate to have both Mr. Swartz and Mr. Coletta. The latter confirmed this point and emphasized that planning and program budgeting could indeed be used as instruments to further the power of budget-makers, but that they *should* be used in the opposite way to encourage people at the program level to develop new ways of delivering services without regard to institutional boundaries.

Dr. Passow's paper updated our thinking on new trends in the educational field. Particularly important was his stress of the importance of relating the formal educational system to the total resources of the community. Dr. Trump reiterated this point and urged the use of the total community and its various facilities, including the library, as tools of education. His critique began to set the stage for some specificity in our thinking about how to open up the public school system, relating it to the community and having it use the community, especially its various library facilities, as resources. This question, of course, addresses itself directly to the matter of coordination of facilities.

Mr. Brong's discussion of library networks underscored the impact of technology in developing both cooperation and coordination among all kinds of libraries. Once this kind of free-flowing network system develops among libraries, we felt that it would be much easier for the educational system to relate itself to the various library resources. Dr. Heinich reinforced all of these points and stressed the necessity for our thinking in terms of an eventual melding of the professions without any fear of one swallowing or threatening the other. Miss Molz's historical perspective reminded us that we are not talking about a new thing when we talk about total community library service. Schools and libraries have historically been mutually reinforcing community agencies, but for the last twenty years both have been rushing headlong into a kind of fragmentation parallel to the sort taking place in the total metropolitan area.

My group would like to stress that there were some important gaps in the papers and that these may not have been adequately covered in our discussions. Kathleen Molz and, particularly, Mildred Frary did talk in some specific detail about the problems of bureaucratic politics, conflicts among agencies, how to relate to deeply entrenched and highly professionalized bureaucracies. The librarians on one hand, with their many splinter groups, and the educators on the other hand, with their many internal frictions and shifting allegiances, are both, in a real sense, entrenched bureaucracies.

Surely this conference ought to encourage more of the kind of cross-professional dialogue that is beginning to occur between the mutual roles of schools and libraries. If we are to confront quite directly, and in a determined way, the question of how we reorganize library services, we have to address, in the first instance, the politics within the professions and the politics between the professions. It is a shame that the American Library Association is still located in Chicago. Some time in the future surely ALA and NEA ought to occupy headquarters in the Washington area jointly so that they can work in concert.

The feeling in our group was very strongly that the professionals who make up the two professions ought to get together and work out their differences at the national level, that they ought to take a concerted position with the Federal government on ways of coordinating their resources. This kind of unified educational thrust ought to provide the basis for governmental policies at all levels. The leadership ought to come from the professions, rather than from federal or state bureaucrats. I think I report accurately when I say that the majority of our group felt that the professions ought to find ways to take the initiative. A minority felt that the two professions could never get together in a unified way in order to provide the basis for leadership. They tended to think that the federal government, through its Office of Education, ought to provide this leadership.

S. Janice Kee (discussion group 2)

I am very much afraid that the terminology we have been using means so many different things to so many different people that we need clarification on what we are talking about when we use them in different settings. If we are not careful, such terms as "community information services" and "community learning centers" are going to fall into the same disreputable condition as the term "library system," which now means practically nothing because it means so many different things in different parts of the country.

I would first like to give you something of my personal impressions of the frame of mind of group 2. The people in this group recognize that there is still a very wide gap to be bridged between theory and practice in the coordination of library services. I think the group believes that there is great urgency in working toward improved ways of delivering library services. But they also feel very keenly the psychological, political, and jurisdictional barriers that must be broken down if this is to be achieved. The recommendations that the group came up with are cautiously expressed, but they are offered as realistic and practical ways of approaching the goal of total community library service. I think also that this group, particularly the teachers and the librarians, leaned very heavily toward placing the responsibility for national leadership upon the professional organizations as distinguished from the Federal government. At the same time, the group recognized that there is great power in the Federal funding agencies through Federal research and development grants and through Federal programs such as NDEA [National Defense Education Act], HEA [Higher Education Act], and LSCA [Library Services and Construction Act]. So, while the group felt that they would much rather see local and professional initiative extended to the utmost in developing community library services, they realize that, to have this happen, it must be written in the national standards and the national goals.

We recommend that the ALA-NEA Joint Committee, the sponsors of this conference, use this conference, and the expertise of the participants, as a launching pad for pushing several things. First, national professional leadership should be asserted in a united way towards solving the problem of making existing information services available to every person in every community. Second, the collection and dissemination of information on pilot projects, experimental programs, etc., must be improved. We need to know not only what is going on, but also how well it is going, what is working and what is not working. It has been pointed out that we are frequently hesitant to tell about what does not work. Yet we need such information since it can provide guidance and direction in other communities. A third recommendation is that this committee, again as the action group, should give concerted attention to developing effective instruments for the evaluation of experimental projects in total community library service. This latter recommendation is related to the need expressed in Mr. Coletta's paper for impact indicators and is not to be interpreted as a call for adoption of any particular total community library model. We are quick to recognize the need for basing any such program on individual community needs.

Nettie Taylor (discussion group 3)

When we began this conference, the question was posed: "Is the present institutional approach the best answer to providing information and learning services to the total community?" In different ways we have explored this question in our discussion group. We may not have answered it directly, but as I look over the notes the recorders took and as I recall what was discussed, I believe some recurring positions and concerns were being expressed throughout all of our discussions, regardless of the particular paper under discussion at the moment.

One of these recurring concerns was: "Do we really know what the library needs of the community are? Have we really established these needs?" For example, and only for example, does the New York State proposal for school-based total library services for children derive from a thorough analysis of weaknesses in the services being provided currently by at least two agencies, or does the "need" in this particular case mean only that the budget authorities, politicians, and administrators are questioning the economic justification of providing services in two different institutions to the same group of children? Sometimes the need to justify our practices or to change our ways may be forced on us from the outside; I think it should rather be something that we see within our own responsibilities as a need to change and improve. I'm not objecting to change or to trying out new organizational patterns. I'm just saying that we should know where the rationale for change is coming from.

Another thing that kept coming out of our group discussions was this: "Are our service goals and our objectives really clear and really definite?" I sensed, for instance, some ambiguity and uncertainty within the group about what responsibility the school or the library has for taking on *all* of society's problems and trying to solve them within the context of an institution. To what degree should it accept responsibility for the mitigation of larger societal problems? There was enough confused feeling within our own group about this topic that I suspect it is one which deserves considerable clarification.

The other main issue that kept recurring in our discussion was that one cannot really talk about total community library service except possibly in a community the size of Olney, Texas, where you are able to see the total picture. Can you really talk about Philadelphia, Washington, D.C., or Baltimore as communities? Or do we have to focus on specific segments of these large aggregations of people, and to focus on a particular point in time, in order to get anywhere with the establishment of needs and the setting of goals?

In our group we tried to look at the various audiences within the community, and we shifted back and forth between thinking about the library needs of young children as students, the library needs of children other than students, and the needs of adults, ranging from the sophisticated information needs of scholars and specialists to the basic information needs for daily living. We were never really able to focus on the problem in any depth unless we had a specific, identifiable group of people, or a community, that we were trying to think about. Without a particular community in mind, it was difficult to look at the various alternatives to the organization of library service, or of learning services, that were being discussed in the conference papers. Much of what was said by Dr. Trump and Dr. Passow was concerned with alternatives. Nobody is yet pushing these alternatives as complete replacements for existing learning environments such as schools and libraries, but the alternatives deserve a sympathetic hearing. We are exploring some of these alternatives right now, but I don't think we can yet come up with recommendations for closing out what we already have. We are not at that stage now, but I hope that at some point we can seriously think about giving up some of the things that we are now doing in order to do other things better.

Then, with the discussion following Kathleen Molz's paper, we finally got a concrete example of a community library project that was actually happening. As you listened to the discussion of the Philadelphia project, some of our themes began to fall into place. The need for the Action Library had been established through careful research, the goals of the project were clear, operating procedures had been devised, and provision had been made for evaluating the impact of the project. With the discussion of that project, the conference came back full circle to the question posed at the beginning. I realize, and I think that the group realizes, that one project is not going to answer all the questions and that we are not going to be able all the time to benefit from the money, and from the kind of research and investigation, that went into the Philadelphia project. But it does seem to me that we can learn many things from this large project. We don't necessarily have to wait for large amounts of money and large amounts of research in order to carry on.

In every discussion, following every paper, the thought was expressed that we need more pilot projects of this type to demonstrate new patterns of community library service. We need to try a lot of different arrangements in a lot of different places, and we need to address the particular needs of many audiences. Only in this way are we going to learn what is really best for the people we are trying to serve. What is right for Olney, Texas, is not right for Philadelphia. The more pilot projects we can encourage, the better able we will be to define total community library service.

Robert Myers (discussion group 3)

I suppose the major reason I am here is because we have coordinated at Miami University fourteen library executive development programs for library administrators. In that capacity I have come to know many librarians quite well and to understand some of their problems. This conference was carefully planned to involve a variety of professional backgrounds and I have enjoyed participating. It was a good idea to bring together such a diversity of opinions and viewpoints. This certainly should provide much ammunition for future planning.

As I heard the reports which preceded this one, I thought that it would be hard for the last person to think of any new things to say. At the risk of being redundant, I would like to bring to you a few ideas from our group. There is a tendency for any person to warp or to twist recommendations in terms of his own thinking. To the members of my group, I want to apologize for any distortion that I may convey.

First, I think we feel that libraries of all kinds should work harder to discover the needs of the publics that they should be trying to meet. What are the goals of the particular library—storing materials, making information available to the public, complementing the resources of other educational institutions, serving a specific age group? Just what are the distinctive needs of the various publics that library is trying to serve? As a participant in marketing research, I think that many of the surveys we do should be done in the library field as well. Where do people get their information? Where do they learn? What medium offers the most impact?

These things must be determined so that we can learn what the public really wants and uses. Then, having found that out, we should set objectives to guide the actions of libraries toward meeting these needs as precisely as possible. These objectives will guide us to such things as the kinds of equipment we should buy, the kinds of services we should offer, the location of outlets, the hours the library should be open, and the extent to which we should try to reach certain audiences which do not respond to standard library services.

Specific objectives should guide our action. We have to make our objectives as specific as possible. I can't stress that too much. Following a conference at the State Library of Ohio last January on management by objective, we went to the Dayton Public Library and picked a department that we thought was one with the least quantifiable objectives. We picked the reference department. I won't go into detail, but the reference librarian and I discovered after working out our objectives together that they could be made much more specific and much more quantifiable than either of us had realized before we started.

Then, we must develop, wherever possible, ways to measure performance against objectives. We decide what services the reference department of a library should be delivering based on the ascertained needs. Having made that decision and set up our objectives, we should then develop quantifiable measures to determine the extent to which we are meeting our objectives. There are many areas in library services where program budgeting can be very effective and should be used. Generally, these are the more quantifiable aspects of library work. Certainly there is no reason why it cannot be used in all of the office operations, such as the acquisition and organization of materials. In areas where the data are quantifiable, I think PPBS or some adaptation should be used. In areas where it is more difficult to quantify, but even yet possible, management by objective is the approach. The director ought to sit down with the department heads and work out as specifically as possible what the reference department or the circulation department or the audiovisual service should be doing.

In our group we felt strongly that the development of community learning centers for total community library service should be urged so that schools, libraries, museums, churches, and the media—all of the educational and informational services—would be coordinated in their approach to educating and informing the various publics of the community. Such a coordinated effort would see to it that each agency is doing what it is best equipped to do. As a method for coordination, we were intrigued with Dr. Trump's idea of the community director of learning resources who would see to it that all community learning activities would be coordinated. There was some apprehension expressed that another level of bureaucracy would just be piled on top of the present bureaucracy. The belief that the more layers, the more difficult the coordination becomes, may or may not be true. I think we felt that this approach was worth trying. Maybe it should be the first project to be tried following this conference. One of us suggested that, short of this, a coordinating policy committee made up of board members or other representatives from the various agencies would be a first step. Such a policy-making committee would have the authority to implement certain policies adopted or at least to direct that they be adopted. We do feel that it would take a strong coordinating agency to put all this together and avoid duplication.

A recommendation which grows out of the paper on technology is that in any total community library effort there should be a recognition of the tremendous power of nonprint media as learning motivators to the young, the underachievers, and the nonreaders of all ages. Use of nonprint media in all educational agencies, and particularly in libraries, should be expanded greatly. The amount of money currently spent by libraries on nonprint, as opposed to print, material is very low. We feel, because of the motivating power and the communication power of the nonprint media, that the balance is out of order and should be changed.

It was our general feeling that education, and all library-related activities, should be more flexible and, in general, made more informal and enjoyable. We applaud every effort to get the educational process out of the stilted, formal atmosphere of schools and libraries, taking it out into the neighborhood and involving all of the resources of the city or the country. Anybody who can make a contribution to the educational process should be involved. Again, multimedia use, with an emphasis on the power of the nonprint media to motivate and reach the young and the illiterate, is essential. Many of us decried the fact that while $.40 of every tax dollar spent by state and local governments for all services goes to the public schools, less than one-half cent goes to library service. Our feeling is that if libraries can find where the greatest unmet educational and informational needs are, if they will set specific objectives for meeting these needs, and if they will develop quantifiable techniques for measuring performance against objectives, they should be able to prove their value, justify their budget requests, and increase their share of the public funds. Innovative approaches to total community library services, which would get away from present rigid institutional frameworks, should be even more likely to attract public support.

James Kitchens (discussion group 4)

Charles Tate, the leader of our discussion group, was extremely consistent throughout all of our meetings in speaking for the right of communities to determine what they wanted in library services. He discouraged what he called a paternalistic outlook where outsiders, such as professionals, come in, in an extremely directive fashion, and tell a community how things are going to be. This theme, of community determination versus professional direction, permeated many of our discussions.

We had a very good group. Ours was the most hard-working of all. We always went beyond the time limits. When everybody else was leaving, we were still hard at work. What did we do with all of that hard work? Rather than give you a blow-by-blow description, I'll pick out two of those highlights from our discussions which have not already been mentioned by others.

We dealt at length with the idea of accountability and with our seeming fear of the concept of accountability. We consoled ourselves with the thought that instruments of empirical evaluation are not yet sophisticated enough to get at the kinds of things that libraries do. We tend to feel that the quality of our work cannot be measured by quantitative instruments and, therefore, we are afraid of those persons in control who would decide our fiscal fate on the basis of them.

We also, implicitly at least, reckoned with the fear that maybe we are not doing such a good job after all and that these instruments, when sophisticated enough, will really get at the quality of our work, only to find that it is not very high. We may be a little like the farmer who rejected a subscription to a farming magazine on the basis that he was not farming as well as he knew how already and did not need to be told about it. Maybe librarians are in the same situation. We are afraid of accountability because accountability means that our sins will become evident to those outside.

We talked about libraries as a part of community learning resources, as part of the total education force, not so much formal education in the sense of the three Rs, but informally by the provision of information, data, learning experiences, and recreational reading to people in the community.

We talked at great length about the necessity for recognizing that we deal not with one community at a time but with many stratified communities within even a small city. Each of these communities has specific kinds of needs.

We talked a great deal about whether or not the members of the various strata recognize what their needs are. Here is where our concern with community determination came to the surface again. What right do we, as members of a professional library and education community, have to look at other groups and say to them that they do not know what they need? Yet, at the same time, others in our group supported strongly the idea that librarians had a kind of advocacy role to play. Librarians should say, "You know *some* of your needs, but you don't know *all* of your needs, let us therefore expand your horizon so that you see beyond the level at which you now exist."

We talked also about the pragmatics of trying alternatives to old delivery systems, the fact that there are endless problems—legal, administrative, vested interest problems—that keep us from even seeing what we need to do. And yet we came around at the end of our discussion to realize that we really don't have enough hard data about these problems. For too long we have indulged in conferences and dialogues such as this, kicking around opinions. Maybe it is time to open ourselves up to research that could answer, on an empirical basis, whether or not the things that we talk about are possible. We applaud all efforts to collect hard data and to make it available so that our subjective opinions can be corrected by objective facts.

Charles Tate (discussion group 4)

The deliberations of group 4 were well summarized by James Kitchens. I would like to take a little time to develop one or two other ideas which are really not necessarily recommendations of the group.

I get the feeling that librarians, be they in the public sector or in a school system, feel somehow that they are not being included in many of the new directions, that they want to improve the quality of their services, and have lots of good ideas about how to proceed, but that the initiative is being taken from them. They want to enhance their profession, they want to relate to community needs, they really want to do all of the things that we have talked about here. But I sense a great deal of frustration and a feeling of isolation that tend to exclude them from some of the processes by which new developments arrive in community activities. The librarians seem more than willing to experiment. They would like very much to see some of the traditional kinds of library agencies given enough research and development money to try out some of these so-called new approaches. They would like to experience first hand and learn for themselves how to modify and change staff and services. In all of our discussions there was a very strong feeling within the group that initiative and resources were being given to other entities at the state and local level and that they, the library agencies most closely involved, were not being included.

There are several other points that I would like to raise. There is a great disparity in the level of information resources of all types available in affluent and in poor communities. The poor communities should be provided with a range of information and program materials comparable to those that are available to the more affluent families and communities. The new technologies discussed in Brong's paper, such as cable television and video cassettes, can help make this information delivery service to all parts of the community possible. Through technological means a uniform information delivery system can be developed that does not favor the well-to-do. This could be done with the technology available today. Libraries can play a very significant role in this because certain kinds of material simply will not be available from commercial channels. They must be publicly provided. The present distribution system is not yet adequate to handle this kind of programming nor is the program content yet here. Cable television and the development of video cassettes will lead to the availability of all kinds of educational programming but only those with money will be able to get at it unless the public libraries do something.

On the issue of coordination of the delivery of library services at the community level, I think it is important that librarians accept some responsibility for helping to develop political consciousness among minority groups and among the poor by involving them in decision-making. In the urban centers in particular there are rapid shifts in population. These have led to a breakdown in the sense of community. It takes a long time to recreate community sensibility. In the present atmosphere of emerging political aspirations, the control functions of library services—as of other services—will inevitably be decentralized. Out of this decentralization process the service needs of the particular communities will emerge. There has to be an understanding on the part of librarians of the social, political, and psychological dynamics of undeveloped, underdeveloped, and politically oppressed groups. While there are many common interests, goals, and aspirations among the people of these groups, a community does not yet really exist—if a community is defined as an integrated decision-making unit within which issues can be resolved without destructive conflict. It is important to realize that, in most of our major cities, community in this sense does not now exist but is evolving, is emerging. It is vital that such a community be involved in some measure in the control of its institutions and their resources.

Finally, on the issue of accountability, I don't think there is any question that, as public institutions, libraries must be accountable to all segments of the public. Libraries of all types involved in the resource allocation process must recognize that institutional racism, segregation, and other historical practices have caused significant differences between the information resources available to minorities and to the white majority. The information resources available in ghettos, barrios, and reservations are quite different from that available in affluent white suburbs. Great differences exist also in the needs of such disadvantaged groups for information services. Unless these differences are recognized, such communities will never adequately be served, PPBS notwithstanding. If the objective of total community library service is merely to provide a uniform level of service to all sectors of the community, then the disadvantaged communities will remain in a relatively undeveloped state since their distinctive needs will not be served. Accountability to disadvantaged communities means more than evening out the allocation of resources. It has to do with a willingness to share the planning, policy-making, and decision-making process with these groups directly. They have so long been excluded from such affairs that they need to be retrained in a sense of community. In simple terms, I am talking about sharing of power.

FORMAL RECOMMENDATIONS

The Conference on Total Community Library Service, held on May 11-13, 1972, under the sponsorship of the Joint Committee of the American Library Association and the National Education Association agreed that there is an urgent need for coordination of all library services and resources at the community level in order to provide maximum service to users.

This need grows out of a larger need for sweeping changes in our present way of handling education and the exchange of information, changes that may well require the replacement of some parts of our present delivery system with newer and more flexible user-oriented systems.

This reformation of education and of library service will not come about easily. It will meet with inertia and resistance from within and without. However, the Conference agreed that the initiative for change and self renewal can best come from the professionals involved and that the responsibility lodges with them, not with governmental authorities.

The Conference proposed no single format for the coordination of community library services, recognizing that diversity is important and that careful study of local conditions and local needs should determine the forms of coordination.

With these general principles in mind, the Conference on Total Community Library Service addresses the recommendations below to the leadership of the American Library Association and the National Education Association, to constituent units of these associations, and to other groups interested in education and library services whose cooperation is essential if coordination of community library services is to become a reality.

I. We recommend that the American Library Association and the National Education Association jointly and officially sponsor research and pilot projects on the coordination of school, public, and other library services at the community level. These projects should be carefully planned and objectively evaluated. The results should be widely disseminated not only to the professions involved but to community decision makers and local governmental officials.

II. We urge continued exploration of the concepts of a community coordinating council and of a community coordinator of library and learning resources. A feasibility study should be undertaken as a preliminary to possible projects aimed at setting up such coordinating councils in representative communities.

III. We recommend that in designing, executing, and evaluating multiagency library service projects, the cooperating agencies make full use of the methodologies already developed in planning, political science, sociology, and that representatives from these fields be included as members of multidisciplinary task forces.

IV. We urge librarians in all types of libraries to involve themselves aggressively as resource agents and as program consultants to the many efforts now underway that seek to develop alternative patterns for education at all levels from pre-school to the open university. Librarians need close contact with these movements as surely as they do with the formal educational establishment.

V. We urge teachers in all types of educational programs to make maximum use of all community information resources in their own teaching and to lend their individual support to community efforts at coordination of such resources across institutional lines.

VI. In all stages of the coordination of community library services and the development of multiagency projects, we urge that there be the widest possible community involvement. This is especially important in areas with large proportions of low income and minority residents, where the development of a sense of community responsibility for decision making and goal setting is an urgent necessity.

VII. In all efforts at coordination of library and learning resources to serve the community better, we urge that fuller recognition be given to the power of nonprint media, and especially to the motivational power of nonprint media for those unable to use print easily. The budget and the programs of service proposed for multiagency efforts should make substantial commitment to nonprint resources.

VIII. Recognizing the general inadequacy of tools and techniques now available for measuring the impact of library service, and seeing such measurement as a critical need if libraries are to compete successfully for public funding, we urge that researchers and funding agencies interested in better library service give high priority to the problem of developing, or adapting, impact indicators that do a better job of measuring both in quality and quantity of library service.

IX. Since planning, evaluation, and accountability are increasingly stressed at all levels of government, we urge that high priority be given in continuing education efforts by library schools, state library agencies, and professional associations, to the training and retraining of librarians in applications to library service of such tools of management as planning-program-budgeting and management by objective. The need for such training is critical for all those who manage libraries but especially so for those who are involved in developing coordinated multiagency efforts.

X. Recognizing the great impact of Federal funding on the establishment of innovative programs such as multiagency library service, we urge that the leaders of ALA and NEA concerned with Federal relations work jointly to see that legislation, as well as the implementation of legislative action, reflects clearly what the professions see as priorities in education and library service.

XI. We recommend that the professional associations most closely involved with the provision of library and information resources to the community—ALA and NEA in particular—seek to develop much closer ties at the local and state levels so that a concerted voice may be heard by governmental officials responsible for legislation and the implementation of legislation.

XII. We direct the attention of the U.S. Office of Education to the great need for prompt dissemination of the results of research and demonstration projects through the ERIC system. If the results of these projects are to have maximum impact on the field, the research findings must not simply be buried in research reports but must be re-written and made easily available in a form usable by practitioners.

XIII. We urge that appropriate committees, or individual researchers, building on the proceedings of this Conference, synthesize the material now available on the emerging concept of total community library service, gather fuller data on present and planned examples of multiagency library service, establish definition of terms, and describe emerging patterns of organization and service.

XIV. So that programs of library service developed within a community can reflect user needs rather than professional conceptions of user needs, we encourage all efforts at market research directed at discovering what the community actually wants from libraries and how people use libraries.

XV. We urge that appropriate committees of ALA and NEA explore the impact that the emergence of multiagency library and learning centers will have on the education of personnel who will staff these centers. An inventory of competencies would be useful so that deficiencies in present curricula for teacher education and library education can be identified and corrected.

APPENDIX A

Background
Reading on Total
Community
Library Service

JOYCE POST

GROWTH OF AN IDEA

The idea is not new. One could even trace it back to the ancient Greek agora, which in turn influenced the development of the Roman forum, where public discussion, the buying and selling of books, informal meetings, and formal oratory all occurred in a lively community "place."

Fifty years ago Americans were writing about organizing community centers to "broaden the basis of unity among men, to multiply their points of contact, to consider those interests which all have in common" (Jackson, p. 15). The school was to be the parent organization, with a branch of the public library, an art gallery, a music and festival center, motion picture theater, recreation center, an employment bureau, and a public health office all being established within the school building (Ward). Educators still feel that the school is the logical base of operations because "it is the only institution commonly owned by the people . . . it is unbiased and neutral in its relationship to all citizens" (Totten, p. 412).

Libraries also claim a similar role. The concluding statements of a study of the role of the library in the 1970s are: "If we are to survive as a free society . . . people must be helped to think rationally and to maintain their perspectives. Libraries are better fitted than any other agency we now have to do the job" (Mathews and Lacy, p. 44). Herein lies the first problem in any interprofessional cooperation aimed at achieving total community library service.

Joyce Post is a bibliographical assistant, Graduate School of Library Science, Drexel University, Philadelphia, Pennsylvania.

COMMUNITY SCHOOLS

The idea of school-based community educational services got underway in the 1930s, the prime mover being the highly motivated immigrants then flocking to America. From the beginning there were different philosophies on how to go about community education. The oldest takes the centralized approach; all community activities, except the religious, should take place within the school. One of the best examples of this type of community school is found in Flint, Michigan (C. Campbell). The decentralized approach holds that the community itself provides the best sources for education. This idea is very popular now in both high schools and colleges; Philadelphia's Parkway School is probably the best known (Bremer; Cox).

In the "lighted schools," those characterized by the Flint example above, the activities for adults are called adult education and appear to be mostly middle class; additional vocational training to enable one to rise in one's already existing job, cooking classes for those who already know basic nutrition facts, etc. Despite the War on Poverty, the above conception of adult education still persists, although there is a slow rise of adult basic education centers where one can get job seeking and nutrition facts as well as learn how to read and write.

Many attempts have been made to distinguish between adult education and community education. Minzey and LeTarte feel the difference lies in goals and objectives: adult educators develop programs with the basic purpose of individual improvement, while community educators use these programs as a springboard to social action; to involve the community in the decision-making process.

Another educator feels that the only distinction can be that adult education is limited to adults and community education includes everyone. He realizes this vagueness, and points out that terms like continuing education and community development confuse the field even more (Jensen). In addition to pointing out the problems of definition, Jensen also points out the lack of or need for more cooperation. These problems of definition and cooperation recur constantly throughout all the literature examined for this study.

The *Community Education Journal* is the best publication for keeping up with the current happenings in community schools and the community education movement. There are frequent descriptions of centers, although rare indeed is any mention of a learning center for adults and young adults, and there are many articles relating community education to community development.

SOCIAL SERVICE CENTERS

The settlement idea of participating in the social welfare of a community by enlisting the cooperation of local people got its start in the United States in 1886. In 1960 a comprehensive study was made of over 125 settlements and neighborhood centers. In addition to examining the usual services to families, older people, young people, retarded people, etc., the study takes a look at those centers having a policy of cooperation with public agencies (Hillman).

The idea of one-stop, multiservice neighborhood centers got its biggest boost with the Economic Opportunity Act of 1964. These centers are designed to do the following:

1. Provide information and referral services to help people use established agencies
2. Act as advocate to protect a client's interests and rights with respect to another agency
3. Provide concrete services directly to individuals and families
4. Organize and mobilize groups for collective action on behalf of neighborhood residents.

Some of these projects are well known: Community Progress, Inc. of New Haven, HARYOU-ACT of Central Harlem, and Mobilization for Youth also of New York City (Perlman, p. 1).

The centers provide these services on three levels of need:

1. Basic necessities of urban living (housing, income, education)
2. Helping services (legal aid, job counseling)
3. Facilitating services to utilize available benefits (information and referral services).

It is recommended that the facilitating services are best provided under auspices that are separate and neutral with respect to other agencies. They are of use to all citizens and should not be identified with just the poor, the sick, or the aged as the basic and helping services usually are (Perlman, p. 79).

Centers are usually torn between two strategies in their planning philosophy: that of providing services, or of organizing residents for social action to change local conditions and obtain better services. Beyond a certain point, a professional finds his work becoming primarily political (Harvey and Heiny; Perlman). Perlman feels this linking of services and social action is an important innovation, particularly in publicly supported agencies (p. 74).

During the Johnson Administration, a demonstration project involving multiservice centers in fourteen cities was jointly administered by three federal departments—HUD, HEW, and Labor—and the Office of Economic Opportunity. Attempts at interagency cooperation were a failure on all levels—federal, regional, and neighborhood. Agreement was not forthcoming on priorities—services delivery, community mobilization, and/or opportunities enhancement. The lesson learned by this project, which declined in mid-1969, was that federal and regional coordination should be limited to monitoring, earmarking of funds, and evaluation (Lawson).

One additional problem deserves mention. Within the multiservice framework there is "a strong tendency for each service to maintain its independence. Each has its own professional commitments and language, its status needs, its established patterns of providing services. Each service tends to perceive problems in its own terms and is reluctant to 'surrender' its clients or share them with another service" (Perlman, p. 34).

A concise, up-to-date discussion of neighborhood service centers appears in the *Encyclopedia of Social Work* ("Neighborhood Service Centers"). Lots of people have faith in the center idea. The New York Commissioner of Education's Committee on Library Development says that the joining together of individual educational and social agencies in education parks, community centers, etc., depends primarily on the physical characteristics of the community in question (New York, p. 24).

Louis Levine of San Francisco State College proposed a national network of 400 community centers, and discusses the importance of the "sense of place." He states that funds should come from a single federal source, go directly to the neighborhood resident group responsible for the center, and cover no less than five years in an attempt to avoid the "hope offered/abruptly withdrawn syndrome" (U.S. Congress, pt. 11, p. 2438-44).

In contrast to the above, and in an effort to force solutions to the age-old problems of cooperation, the U.S. Department of Housing and Urban Development's (HUD) Neighborhood Facilities Program requires that cities applying for funds "plan and design the service system with a variety of relevant, state, local, county and private agencies and neighborhood groups" (U.S. Congress, pt. 18, p. 3664). Minneapolis, using this HUD money, found it took almost ten years of working together by the local Board of Education, the Parks and Recreation Board and several private social agencies before the opening of their Charles E. Matthews Neighborhood Center (Soule). A $2.5 million community education center in Flint combines an Elementary Education Services component, a Recreation Services component, and a Community Improvement Services component. Among other things, the latter provides for adult high school classes, adult basic education, community health services, a center for community action and community information dissemination, and a community learning and study center (Nierman).

LIBRARY CENTERS

One of the library profession's answers to the turmoil of the 1960s was increased service outlets in the form of neighborhood library centers. Some are housed in traditional library branches, but depart from traditional library service in programming, philosophy of service, and materials used, while others add the additional important ingredient of informal quarters.

The New Haven Free Public Library's Chapel Street Neighborhood Center, opened in June, 1965, is considered the first of its kind (Brown, pp. 87-96). Investigations of ten such library centers "indicate [that] neither the actual location of the center within the neighborhood or the physical characteristics of the quarters . . . is as important as the 'empathy,' 'openness,' and 'accessibility' of the staff" (National Book Committee, p. 20). More research is needed on what constitutes the neighborhood of a neighborhood library center. Baltimore figures on a five block radius as the limit, while Richmond, Indiana, says no more than three blocks. Library centers are no different from community schools and social service centers in their attempts to give hiring priorities to local residents, and to make use of professionals and specialists drawn from outside their own field.

Few community action agencies, public or private, think of libraries as instruments for change. Only recently have the schools been regarded as such. Because of this, library attempts to seek interagency cooperation at the planning stage are largely unsuccessful, although at the programming level, cooperation is more common. Statewide interagency cooperation occurred when the State Library of Ohio and the Ohio Bureau of Employment Services worked together to make library materials available to job seekers (Shubert and Dowlin). Because of the large number of middle class "new hungry" in the Seattle area, the King County Library System uses some of its branches as certification outlets for the USDA Food Stamp program. Librarians found that it took much persistence to bring the local public assistance officials around to the idea that library facilities could be useful in such a program (Griffen).

Cooperation, or rather the lack of cooperation, works the other way, too. In at least two instances neighborhood libraries have been started by social workers instead of librarians. The Alley Library, located in five basement rooms in a Washington, D.C., brownstone, waited three years before formalizing a relationship with the District of Columbia Public Library, which now provides additional books and part-time staff for cataloging (Harre). The South Center Library, located in a storefront in San Francisco, has no connection with the San Francisco Public Library, but is backed instead by a Neighborhood Legal Assistance Foundation and a Police Community Relations group. Complementing its "down home" atmosphere is a wood-burning stove, a coffee urn, and two cats ("Slum Storefront").

In a South Boston Housing Project the residents have started their own library, located, along with twenty other agencies, in a multiservice center occupying twelve apartments in a wing of one of the project buildings. The library coordinator, prior to taking up that volunteer position, was a special librarian. She feels that the primary jobs connected with a community-owned library, such as cooperating with other community resources, sorting out donated material, publicizing the library, training staff, and acquainting the community with resources, fall more within the frame of reference of a special librarian than of a public librarian (see also Monroe). She warns against one problem of libraries in multiservice centers: other professionals working there will turn to the library to serve their own professional needs. The primary purpose of serving the community must be recognized by all. If the library does agree to collect some professional material (a good way to keep interprofessional communications open), then guidelines must be explicitly drawn up and clearly adhered to (Spence).

High John, a library operated in a house in a deprived area near Washington, D.C., as a laboratory for University of Maryland students studying library service to the disadvantaged, was considered a success in its programming and community relations. But when it came to the more basic problems of determining: (1) the limits of the library's role as both a social action agency and a middle-class institution, and (2) what research needs to be done to find effective ways to serve disadvantaged groups, answers were not forthcoming (Moon; Geller; Moses).

INFORMATION CENTERS

Many of the library centers just described attempt to gather and disseminate information about community resources. However, *the* major study on the subject, done by the Columbia University School of Social Work, does not consider the library's role in information worth mentioning (Kahn). Librarians should view with some alarm a later statement by Kahn: "Libraries were not visible as information resources at any point in our empirical work" (National Book Committee, p. 24).

While Kahn's study was made within the context of information relating to social welfare and public service, the call is out for libraries to respond as information resources in a big way (Bundy). The Enoch Pratt Free Library in Baltimore (Donohue and Peppi) and the Free Library of Philadelphia (Luce) have begun to provide community information services on a clearinghouse basis, and the University of Maryland Library School provided a beginning in library education for a subspeciality in this kind of work (Welbourne). In a survey made in 1967 for the National Advisory Commission on Libraries to determine how libraries were being affected by social change and how they might also effect it, one respondent felt that "the resources required by our information needs transcend our present definitions of libraries." He hypothesized the establishment of "a centralized information base (representing a variety of public services) so that individuals, however uninformed, can satisfy their major information needs in a single place." Libraries must "grasp the significance of this opportunity—it will not fall automatically into their laps—or other, possibly more inexperienced but highly motivated groups, may capitalize upon it instead" (quoted in Lacy and Mathews, pp. 79-80).

In the past few years a new type of alternative organization, known by various names: drop-in center, crisis center, HELP, etc., has sprung up in a great number of places. While their services are directed mostly to young people with drug or suicide problems, these hotlines and switchboards are fulfilling a community need which libraries need to take into consideration in planning total community service (Forsman).

The seventeenth annual Allerton Park Institute, sponsored by the University of Illinois, Graduate School of Library Science, was devoted to libraries and neighborhood information centers. The proceedings of this Institute were not available for examination at the time this survey was made.

LEARNING CENTERS

When they hear the term "learning center," most educators and librarians think of it as a relatively new term applied chiefly to school libraries that acquire the nonprint media now inundating and revolutionizing the field of education. No longer is learning oriented only to print and to the classroom. As more and more of the new technology allows for individual learning, so will the term "learning center" or "resource center" be more and more applied to any library of any size or type.

Learning centers are based on the concept that the library is a place where learning occurs, rather than where learning materials are stored. "Stress is laid on the moving of information to the student, not on the collecting of information. The role of the teacher changes from teaching to managing learning so that the student learns how to gain knowledge" (Hicks and Tillin, p. 4). In this sense the whole school becomes the learning center. A media center is "a learning center in a school where a full range of print and audio-visual media, necessary equipment, and services from media specialists are accessible to students and teachers" (quoted in Hicks and Tillin, p. 5).

Now the idea of the learning center is being taken out of the school and into the community. The avoidance of the word "library" is done with purpose: it seems hopelessly forever associated with the middle class, and is thought of as a formal, authoritarian, and, therefore, fearful institution. The black community involved in the planning of the Phillis Wheatley Community Library in Rochester, New York, asked specifically that it not be designated a branch of the Rochester Public Library (Molz).

In addition to being the best example of a community learning center, Philadelphia's Action Library (best described by Kathleen Molz's paper in these proceedings; Benford; and L. Martin) represents a very rare example of successful interprofessional cooperation between school and library agencies from the planning stage to the actual demonstration.

At the present time the amount of literature dealing with community learning centers is small. Brief mention of the concept is turning up in increasing numbers of documents (Dordick, p. 106-12; Holt, pp. 227-28), but these proceedings represent its first major treatment.

EXAMPLES FROM LIBRARIANSHIP

Two common denominators in all definitions of librarianship are people and information/knowledge; knowledge being what one has after information has been digested. It is precisely the growth in these areas of population and information that have contributed so much to present day social changes. A third factor, the rise of non-book technology—programmed instruction and other means for individual learning, audio and video tape, direct channel television —also has implications for libraries which want to change their role to that of community resource center (Lacy and Mathews, pp. 1-26).

The former Deputy Director of the Chicago Public Library frequently speaks out concerning library irrelevance to the community and the need for a new conception of the library on a community level. He says: "We have been very busy; we have plunged into the ocean of social change . . . . Viewed by librarians our efforts loom large. Viewed by the people—we are not viewed by the people" (Freiser, 1971). He would like to see libraries thinking of themselves in vastly larger terms than at present. "Education and information are part of the hot core of community regeneration" (Freiser, 1970). He suggests that the public library replace the school library (Freiser, 1967). Just the opposite idea was proposed by the New York Commissioner of Education's Committee on Library Development. In a highly controversial move, this group recommended that all library service to children be taken out of the hands of the public library and be given to school libraries (New York, p. 25). Most librarians will probably think Freiser's dream too vast and vague for action now: "The public library in terms of personal choice, civil liberties, educational potential, and especially style may become the chief free comprehensive educational agency in our society" (Freiser, 1971).

The head of Information, Media and Library Planners of Toronto, sees the public library becoming a multimedia community resource center open to all, "service oriented and not curators of the book" (Bowron). Public library laws would be replaced by public information laws. The information reservoir would exist to supply pressure when needed; the institution would take on advocacy roles.

Lowell Martin also sees branch libraries serving their localities as "a center for the common lives of their people" (L. Martin, 1969, p. 17). The standards for programs in such centers would be adapted to each locality with some branches being information centers, others being cultural centers, and still others being media centers (p. 107). In setting up a self-teaching center depending primarily on nonbook materials for systematic study by young people, Martin recommends followup study to assure that learning centers are just that and not an "amusement stop" (p. 41). One doesn't have to look hard to find more of this handwriting on the wall and for specific ideas about the future role of libraries and librarians (Anderson; Blasingame; Conant; Lacy and Mathews, pp. 1-3, 59-63; Mathews and Lacy, pp. 39-44; New York, p. 24; Owens; Roberts; and E. Smith).

Mathews and Lacy (1970) remind us not to forget that: " 'Libraries will need to provide for reflection, meditation, appreciation, and breathing space for the spirit.' Protecting and nurturing the right of the individual to find out for himself will remain a prime responsibility of the 'people-oriented' as opposed to the 'information-oriented' library" (p. 38).

Attempts have been made to determine whether each specific instance of library use by an individual contributes either to the collective public good of society or only to that individual's personal interest. Discussions quickly become heated, but one library researcher has been brave enough to conclude that when public monies are involved, libraries should direct their resources toward educational activities and not toward recreation functions (Goddard). Contrast this with the above quotation, and with the many answers to the National Advisory Commission on Libraries' survey that see libraries of the future as "cultural service stations" where the rising importance of "recreation, humanistic culture, and leisure" are considered.

As pointed out earlier, the theme of cooperation pervades the literature. In times of economic squeeze, governments and people are insisting new ways be thought of so that resources are carefully used to avoid unnecessary duplication (Brown, pp. 51-73; Goddard; and Legg). Serious thinking concerning school and public library cooperation has been going on for a decade *(Towards a Common Goal)*. Recent changes in society have begun to break down traditional definitions of the functions of public and school libraries. The school librarian who feels that "the library of the future will be the central focal point of the instructional process" (quoted in Lacy and Mathews, App. p. 67) and the public librarian who sees the growth of "Large media complexes [that] will serve all types of patrons without designation as public . . ." (quoted in Lacy and Mathews, App. p. 61) should probably be working together in the same institution.

EXAMPLES FROM EDUCATION

The problems in education are not unlike those of librarianship, except that educators have the added responsibility of being asked to be the primary vehicle for solving the social problems of our time. With their alternative institutions of free schools (Kozol), minischools (Divoky) and street academies (Baines and Young), they have tried to become neighborhood education centers where relevant instruction can take place on a more humanized, individualized level (Gross).

The large educational park concept is just the opposite of the small neighborhood learning center. To eliminate racial segregation, all grade levels from the community at large would go to school in one location. The park would also serve as the educational, cultural, and recreational center for the community as a whole, and it would be economical because common facilities, including the library, would not have to be duplicated (Fernandez; Pettigrew).

The Demonstration Cities and Metropolitan Development (Model Cities) Act of 1966 is another attempt to try to get agencies to plan together to improve ghetto situations. Here too, thinking is along the usual lines; that the school is the most accessible resource in the community and that it should be the coordinating unit for all agencies involved. Also it serves as a model agency of social change, and insures relevant policy and practices on the part of all involved agencies. R. Campbell presents a good cross section of all the ideas and problems inherent in the movement to rejuvenate the inner cities through the schools.

A 1970 Wisconsin Governor's Commission on Education proposed a state Open Education System. It would provide a system of education for all people of the state from cradle to grave, and would draw upon established public and private educational institutions, business, government, industry, and libraries for its major resources. It would emphasize cooperative programming, identification of new audiences, new mixes of professional and technical knowledge in developing programs, the use of existing facilities and communications, and the design of instructional activities of a multisensory nature. Endorsement has generally not been forthcoming. The establishment asks: Where will the money come from? Who will control the Open School? Won't existing programs do the job if better funded? Questions arise regarding whether there really are population groups not adequately served by present programs (Wedemeyer and Ghatala).

The President of the Academy for Educational Development in New York City proposes a Commission on Education in every urban area which would make a community inventory of all educational resources, develop a master plan for the use of these resources by all, and develop new types of educational programs to fill in gaps (Eurich). On the other hand, Doll suggests that elementary and secondary schools have sometimes accepted responsibility for too much within the larger context of education; other agencies might well completely take over some aspects of education. McLuhan and Leonard see education in the global village being "more concerned with training the senses and perceptions than with stuffing brains" (p. 113). "The walls between school and world will continue to blur" (p. 114).

What do students themselves say? They feel "that most of the learnings they now consider important have come to them by way of media and influences outside institutional settings. . . . Stop attempting to compete with and to destroy what we learn elsewhere. Instead, seek to coordinate what we are taught in school with what we learn outside school" (Doll, pp. 39-92).

EXAMPLES FROM ACADEMIA

Most of what academic institutions are doing falls into what is called "community service" and "community development." Tutorial programs for elementary and secondary school students are common. For example, the University of Wisconsin-Milwaukee, is operating a storefront campus in a Puerto Rican, Mexican-American community ("Community Service Programs"). There are conscientious efforts to assure that in such programs the institution is not perceived by the community as a one-way donor, willing to help on its own terms only. Examples of symbiotic trade-offs, in which both community and institution benefit, are given in Spiegel.

The University Year for ACTION is a Federal antipoverty program incorporating many of the ideas of VISTA. University students earn credit by living in the community; they work under established community sponsoring agencies on assignments related to their major courses of study. The idea is evolving into the granting of academic credit for community service without regard to whether the individual performs that service under the auspices of an institution of higher learning (Blatchford).

In Britain, a higher education is still thought of as being just for the elite. But Britain's Open University, which accepts only students twenty-one years or older, requires no formal entry qualifications, and has no full-time students or students on a campus, is an attempt to bring higher education to everyman. Students give approximately fourteen hours a week to home-based, self-instruction via television and radio, student assignments graded by computer, and face-to-face tutoring. One week's attendance on campus is required for each course. The country is divided into twelve regions for administrative purposes and overall there are more than 250 local study centers, usually in universities, technical colleges, or schools. "Underuse of study centers must be regarded as one of the least successful aspects of the university's work" (P. Smith). The University produces a graduate at about 20 percent of the cost of a conventional university graduate.

A similar programming mode occurs in the United States, too.

Large cities such as Chicago (Zigerell) give such degrees through large college systems with regular campuses. A program in Maryland is unique, in that three community colleges, two from Baltimore County and one from Baltimore City, were able to work together with a state supported educational television station to offer four courses at one time beginning in the fall of 1970. Four hundred students officially registered and 600 obtained the study guides from the television station without officially registering. Courses were offered on Monday through Thursday, 6:15 to 7 P.M. and 10:30 to 11:15 P.M. and on Saturdays and Sundays from 9:15 A.M. to noon. Attrition was not a problem; the location of appropriate previously developed courses was the biggest problem (Cohen).

Community colleges are in a strategic position for community development, having full acceptance in the higher education enterprise, coupled with a community orientation. There is still much unrealized potential here. Three Michigan community colleges formed a consortium to expand the community services concept among community colleges. Students and faculty identify community resources and needs during a planning period, and then implement these through both individual and community development programs. In the latter case, they find themselves becoming social advocates (thereby risking bringing the college and community into conflict) in bringing about purposive community change (Raines and Myran).

EXAMPLES FROM ADULT EDUCATION

A study of adult education made in 1965 in the United States is still quite relevant. Of the ten problems identified and their accompanying recommendations, four are worthy of mention:

1. Considerable confusion exists over terms used and standardization is needed immediately. A look at the philosophies of community education and adult education shows them to be almost identical.

2. Experimentation with innovation and new institutional forms is needed. Three different kinds of interrelated urban educational institutions were found to be necessary: (a) A community learning and knowledge center for central planning, counseling, clearinghouse, program development, information storage and retrieval, mass media programming and for use as a research and evaluation base. (b) Neighborhood and suburban learning centers tied to community centers through communications technology, with inner city centers on this level tied to community action programs. (c)

Satellite residential centers for intensive learning experiences away from the usual environment.

3. Adult education must begin extensive use of new educational technology.

4. For cooperation and coordination, an Interagency Committee on Adult Education must be established at the federal level, and joint planning on state and local levels must be promoted (Liveright).

For adult educators, there is the fear that the adult evening school might be overshadowed, or even absorbed, by the community college. To avoid this conflict, careful thought must be given to the role of each type of institution, with respect to a comprehensive program suited to meet the needs of all the adults in the community. Specific programs may be found to be better suited to one or the other institution. Extensive cooperation is necessary (Niemi).

EXAMPLES FROM ARCHITECTURE AND CITY PLANNING

In terms of this survey, the library plan for the new town of Columbia, Maryland, done seven years ago seems to miss some of the exciting possibilities of the new towns concept. Perhaps this is because planning had to be done to include the already existing Howard County school and library systems. The new town is organized on three population levels: neighborhoods of 500 to 600 families, villages of 2,500 to 3,000 families, and the town center. Only services for children are planned for on the neighborhood level: an elementary school, a nursery school, a kindergarten, and child care centers. Village centers still combine the libraries of junior and senior high schools and a public library branch in overlapping, but not merged, facilities. The town center will have a main library, a community college, and an adult academy, but library planning for the latter is vague, in that it was not even sure if the academy would have its own collection of materials (Stone).

Fort Lincoln New Town (FLNT), with 4,500 low to middle income housing units planned for a 335 acre site within the city limits of Washington, D.C., is seen as an educational community. All residents are involved in learning and in teaching each other. Five learning complexes, all connected by minirail, will provide for 2,500 students, age five to eighteen, and, in addition, will have early childhood learning centers. At least thirteen different kinds of special learning centers, one of which is an educational resource center for the entire community, will be situated throughout FLNT in commercial facilities. One of the tasks of FLNT is to develop a mechanism for determining and connecting community and regional resources with learning activities and behavioral objectives (Fantini and Young).

Lieberman takes a look at the implications for education of the new cities concept. In some new cities, community facilities are planned to meet the needs of students, whereas in other cases the school facilities are made available to the community. In addition to the semantics, Lieberman points out differences in control and in politics involved. He suggests that communal study halls be built into new apartment buildings. And he deplores the fact that only private enterprise, and these only in a small way, have availed themselves of the $500 million in loan guarantees available through Title VII of the Housing and Urban Development Act of 1970 to both private and public developers of new communities.

The Sternbergs, an architecture-planning-sociology team, have taken a look at contemporary community centers all over the world, complete with many photographs and plans—the school as a community center, settlement houses, recreation centers, centers for the elderly, shopping centers, youth centers, student unions, and the community-centered college. They feel it is impossible to come up with any single theory of how to locate, build, and program a successful community center, since circumstances vary, and so does what is perceived as the major problems and desirabilities of an age. They recommend the following:

1.   When assembling the group which will work together on a new center, seek out the most creative, imaginative, "in-touch" people.
2.   Avoid all standards, since they always have built-in assumptions about what the community is going to need.
3.   Stay open minded. The primary limitation of planning for centers is one of ideas, not money.
4.   Choose a creative, innovative architectural firm (pp. 151-55).

Without resorting to standards, attempts have been made to identify certain organizational principles which are valid from one community to another, and to generalize pattern relationships within the multiservice center concept. Sixty-four individual patterns have been identified. For example, if there is a multiservice center, then it should contain an unmanned self-service area containing all of the basic information required by people who need help (pattern no. 21). If there is such a self-service area, then there should be a flow to: (1) a manned self-service progression area which tells what services are available in the multiservice center and invites people to make use of them (pattern no. 27), and/or (2) a self-service program containing a library, language labs, teaching machines, typewriters, direct tie-in phones to all those services in the larger community not represented in the center, and information in the form of lists and displays (pattern no. 60) (Alexander).

SOME PROBLEMS OF DEFINITION

What constitutes the community or neighborhood of an agency (Warren)? How will such an organization be affected when that community becomes a global village (Childers)? How can the similarities between library service, continuing education, general education, adult education, and community education be maximized? Would it be worthwhile for the practitioners in each to work together rather than try to build up their own separate disciplines?

What is the appropriate use of the terms library, learning center, community resource center, community information center? How can ambiguous nomenclature be avoided? Institutions which might want to call themselves community study centers, for example, should know that social scientists use this very term for places where they conduct studies of a community.

SOME PROBLEMS OF PROFESSIONALISM

How are the aims, objectives, roles, and priorities of the professions involved being changed by present social forces and by a general lack of funds? Should the library, for example, be an archival agency, a cultural agency, an information agency, a media agency, or something else? Would it be profitable for the professions to admit that many of their "unique" functions and objectives are really shared by most of them? What groups can (should any?) take upon themselves the task of trying to erase the current "blurred vision," of trying to build something concrete from the plethora of ideas around? Would realistic research on community needs help?

At what point does the educational agency take on advocacy roles? How does the politicized professional reconcile within himself these roles? Assuming community organization has occurred, how does one (can one?) phase out professional leadership and replace it with local leadership?

Has it been wrong to consider the schools the prime agency for effecting community change? Why are libraries not considered by other professional groups as logical agencies to be included in the business of community change? What measuring instruments can be created to demonstrate the value of libraries as social agencies

(Pings)? What is the potential of the community college in this area?

How can the problem that every community agency feels that it is the *one* logical agency upon which to base all community services (with all other agencies clustering around it), be dealt with?

SOME PROBLEMS OF INSTITUTIONAL CHANGE

The hierarchical nature of bureaucracies leads to self-perpetuation and, eventually, to meaninglessness in terms of social change. As technology increases, problems become more complex and require higher levels of expertise in a variety of subspecialities within a bureaucracy. Such specialization has at least two dangers:

1. Basic problems are not dealt with (Fessler).
2. As specialization increases, greater efforts are made to enlarge those coordinating functions which are directed to maintaining the organization, not changing it (Leles).

In addition to the problems at home, field workers or street-level bureaucrats are becoming increasingly competent and yet are left out of the planning process. They work under stress-producing circumstances: available resources are inadequate, work circumstances present clear physical and/or psychological threats, role and job expectations are ambiguous and/or contradictory. Defense mechanisms set in, with these workers ultimately being charged with being insensitive, incompetent, and resistant to change. These ways of reacting to stress have implications for urban bureaucracies in terms of both in-house and public policy (Robbins; Lipsky).

Policies must be decentralized, so that field workers are allowed to use their judgment in setting up their work priorities and are able to respond instantaneously when a community need arises (Monroe).

The Brooklyn Public Library has a community coordinator program in which these workers are freed completely from in-library service and are attached to areas rather than to specific buildings (Nyren, pp. 43-54). The idea of an independent information specialist working outside the confines of institutional support, and the applications of this idea for community analysis and development, were explored in a 1970 Institute on the Floating Librarian in the Emerging Community (Penland).

One librarian suggests three methods, other than the firing and hiring of people, for changing the formal organizational structure of organizations.

1. Introduction of technology to meet new objectives, not to build bureaucratic empires.
2. Changes in shared norms and values, brought about by continuing education of personnel or the bringing in of change agents and other similar types.
3. Planned redesign of the formal organization. Usually this is done only by intuition and/or on a crisis basis (Pings).

Pings' ideas seem quite traditional. Levine summarizes three newer approaches:

1. An emphasis on "development" bureaucracy, rather than rational, efficiency-oriented bureaucracy, where the predominant goal is the "management of change, that is, the direction of efforts to alter the basic pattern(s) of a way of life" (quoted in Levine, p. 331). Berton H. Kaplan is one of the chief proponents of this idea.

2. Authority is allocated to roles according to "functional necessity." First a job or problem is identified. Then the people having the necessary resources to do the work are brought together in a temporary task force, the ad-hocracy of Alvin Toffler (pp. 124-51), which is dissolved when the job is done. C. Martin discusses the implications of this idea for community service agencies.

3. Bureaucracies and primary groups (the community is a primary group) must perform complementary functions rather than work at cross purposes. Bureaucracies are better equipped to handle expert tasks, while the primary group can best handle the nonexpert tasks. The structures of these two groups are contradictory, but the tasks are interdependent. When a community tries to cooperate with or intervene in a bureaucracy, they should do so by various linking mechanisms based on: (a) How close or how distant community and bureaucratic views are on the problem at hand, and (b) What expert and nonexpert tasks are involved. Twelve linking mechanisms, ranging through advocate bureaucracy, use of the indigenous expert, systematic boycott, to single person ad hoc contact are identified (Litwak and others).

Alternative organizations, or self-service groups, have always existed, especially in education. But because of the widening gap between central decision making and social choice, and because many public facilities have not remained relevant, their numbers are increasing. Any public service that allocates resources largely according to what it thinks people should want, but often do not, is a good candidate for substitution by an alternative organization. They take on the role of advocacy planning—the exercise of the planning function on behalf of specified groups (blacks, poor, elderly) formally unrepresented in the planning process, rather than on behalf of a broadly defined public interest. By doing this, they become actively involved in the organization which they substituted and eventually play an active role in controlling their future urban environment (Ballabon).

At the risk of appearing unimaginative, there seem to be two obvious ways to attack the problems unearthed in this survey:

1. Recognize the importance of an interdisciplinary curriculum in the education of professionals (Boll).
2. Take a new look at the value of research. Determine what basic realistic research is needed to help choose among goals and objectives, and plan it very carefully.

BIBLIOGRAPHY

Alexander, Christopher. *A Pattern Language Which Generates Multi-Service Centers.* Berkeley, Calif.: Center for Environmental Structure, 1968.

Anderson, John F. "Who Speaks for the Concerns of Library Service?" *American Libraries*, Dec. 1970, pp. 1062-68.

Baines, James, and William M. Young. "The Sudden Rise and Decline of New Jersey Street Academies." *Phi Delta Kappan*, Dec. 1971, pp. 240-42.

Ballabon, Maurice B. "The Self-Service Group in the Urban Economy." *Journal of the American Institute of Planners*, Jan. 1972, pp. 33-42.

Benford, John Q. "The Philadelphia Project." *Library Journal*, 15 June 1971, pp. 2041-47.

Blasingame, Ralph. "Libraries in a Changing Society." *Library Journal*, 1 May 1972, pp. 1667-71.

Blatchford, Joseph H. "ACTION in the University." *American Education*, Mar. 1972, pp. 37-40.

Boll, John J. "A Basis for Library Education." *Library Quarterly*, Apr. 1972, pp. 195-211.

Bowron, Albert. "Let's Abolish the Public Library." *Canadian Library Journal*, Nov. 1969, pp. 438-39.

Bremer, John, and Michael Von Moschzisker. *The School without Walls.* New York: Holt, 1972.

Brown, Eleanor F. *Library Service to the Disadvantaged.* Metuchen, N.J.: Scarecrow, 1971.

Bundy, Mary Lee. "Urban Information and Public Libraries, a Design for Service." *Library Journal*, 15 Jan. 1972, pp. 161-69.

Campbell, Clyde M. *Toward Perfection in Learning.* Midland, Mich.: Pendell Pub. Co., 1969.

Campbell, Roald, and others, eds. *Education and Urban Renaissance.* New York: Wiley, 1969.

Childers, Thomas. "Community and Library: Some Possible Futures." *Library Journal,* 15 Sept. 1971, pp. 2727-30.

Cohen, Jerry M. "Maryland's Community College of the Air." *Junior College Journal,* Oct. 1971, pp. 33, 36, 40.

Community Education Journal. Midland, Mich.: Pendell Pub. Co. Feb. 1971- (quarterly).

"Community Service Programs." *School and Society,* Feb. 1972, pp. 81-82.

Conant, Ralph W. "Future of Public Libraries, an Urban Expert's Optimism." *Wilson Library Bulletin,* Jan. 1970, pp. 544-49.

Cox, Donald W. *The City as a Schoolhouse: The Story of the Parkway Program.* Valley Forge, Pa.: Judson Press, 1972.

Divoky, Diane. "New York's Mini-Schools, Small Miracles, Big Troubles." *Saturday Review,* 18 Dec. 1971, pp. 60-67.

Doll, Ronald C. "Alternative Forms of Schooling." *Educational Leadership,* Feb. 1972, pp. 391-93.

Donohue, Joseph C., and Carole Peppi. *The Public Information Center Project.* Baltimore: Enoch Pratt Free Library, 1971.

Dordick, J. S., and others. *Telecommunications in Urban Development.* (RM-6069-RC) Santa Monica, Calif.: Rand Corp., 1969.

Eurich, Alvin. "High School, 1980." *NASSP Bulletin,* May 1971, pp. 42-53.

Fantini, Mario D., and Milton A. Young. *Designing Education for Tomorrow's Cities.* New York: Holt, 1970.

Fernandez, Alfred P. "The Educational Park, a Second Look." *Journal of Secondary Education,* May 1970, pp. 223-29.

Fessler, Donald R. "Adult Education's Role in Community Self Renewal." *Adult Leadership,* Dec. 1971, pp. 215-16.

Forsman, Carolyn. "Crisis Information Services to Youth: A Lesson for Libraries?" *Library Journal,* 15 Mar. 1972, pp. 1127-34.

Freiser, Leonard H. "The Civilized Network." *Library Journal,* 15 Sept. 1967, pp. 3001-3.

———— "Community, Library and Revolution." *Library Journal,* 1 Jan. 1970, pp. 39-41.

———— "So (Said the Doctor). Now Vee May Perhaps to Begin. Yes?" *Illinois Libraries,* Feb. 1971, pp. 109-14.

Geller, Evelyn. "This Matter of Media." *Library Journal,* 15 June 1971, pp. 2048-53.

Goddard, Haynes C. "An Economic Analysis of Library Benefits." *Library Quarterly,* July 1971, pp. 244-55.

Griffen, Agnes M. "Libraries and Hunger." *Library Journal,* 15 Oct. 1971, pp. 3287-91.

Gross, Beatrice, and Ronald Gross. *Radical School Reform.* New York: Simon and Schuster, 1969.

Harre, David. "Involvement through Chaos." *D. C. Libraries,* Winter 1970, pp. 3-8.

Harvey, David L., and Robert W. Heiny. "The Teacher as a Social Critic: An Examination of Neighborhood Learning Center Activities." *Peabody Journal of Education,* Jan. 1972, pp. 104-18.

Hicks, Warren B., and Alma M. Tillin. *Developing Multi-Media Libraries.* New York: Bowker, 1970.

Hillman, Arthur. *Neighborhood Centers Today: Action Programs for a Rapidly Changing World.* New York: National Federation of Settlements and Neighborhood Centers, 1960.

Holt, John. *Freedom and Beyond.* New York: Dutton, 1972.

Jackson, Henry E. *A Community Center, What It Is and How to Organize It.* Bulletin, 1918, no. 11. Washington, D.C.: Dept. of the Interior, Bureau of Education, 1918.

Jensen, Glenn. "The Role of Adult Education in Community Education." *Community Education Journal,* Aug. 1971, pp. 10-12.

Kahn, Alfred J., and others. *Neighborhood Information Centers: A Study and Some Proposals.* New York: Columbia University School of Social Work, 1966.

Kozol, Jonathan, *Free Schools. New York: Houghton, 1972.*

Lacy, Dan, and Virginia H. Mathews. *Social Change and the Library, 1945-1980.* Final report of the National Advisory Commission on Libraries. ERIC Document, no. ED 022 483. Washington, D.C.: Dept. of Health, Education and Welfare, Office of Education, Bureau of Research, 1967.

Lawson, Simpson. "The Pitiful History of the Pilot Neighborhood Center Program." *City,* Mar./Apr. 1972, pp. 53-57.

Legg, Jean. "Coordinating Library Services within the Community." *American Libraries,* May 1970, pp. 457-63.

Leles, Sam. "Educational Structure, Is It Capable of Innovation." *Clearing House,* Feb. 1970, pp. 368-72.

Levine, Daniel U. "Concepts of Bureaucracy in Urban School Reform." *Phi Delta Kappan,* Feb. 1971, pp. 329-33.

Lieberman, Myron. "Education in the New Cities." *Phi Delta Kappan,* Mar. 1972, pp. 407-8.

Lipsky, Michael. "Street-Level Bureaucracy and the Analysis of Urban Reform." *Urban Affairs Quarterly,* June 1971, pp. 391-409.

Litwak, Eugene, and others. "Community Participation in Bureaucratic Organizations: Principles and Strategies." *Interchange,* no. 4 (1970), pp. 44-60.

Liveright, A. A. *A Study of Adult Education in the United States.*

Brookline, Mass.: Center for the Study of Liberal Education for Adults at Boston University, 1968.

Luce, Robert J. "The Model Cities Community Information Center." *American Libraries*, Feb. 1971, pp. 206-7.

McLuhan, Marshall, and George Leonard. "Learning in the Global Village." *Radical School Reform*. Edited by Beatrice and Ronald Gross. New York: Simon and Schuster, 1969, pp. 106-15.

Martin, Carl. "Beyond Bureaucracy." *Child Welfare*, July 1971, pp. 384-88.

Martin, Lowell A. *Library Response to Urban Change: A Study of the Chicago Public Library*. Chicago: American Library Assn., 1969.

———— "The Philadelphia Project: The Action Library, Its Purpose and Program." Revised; photo-offset (Philadelphia: Philadelphia Student Library Project, 15 Mar. 1972).

Mathews, Virginia H., and Dan Lacy. *Response to Change, American Libraries in the Seventies*. Indiana Library Studies, Report no. 1. Bloomington, 1970.

Minzey, Jack, and Clyde LeTarte. "Community Education, From Program to Process." *Community Education Journal*, Aug. 1971, p. 8.

Molz, Kathleen. "Halfway Houses to Learning." *American Education*, May 1972, pp. 21-23.

Monroe, Margaret E. "Reader Services to the Disadvantaged in Inner Cities." *Advances in Librarianship*. Vol. 2. Edited by Melvin J. Voigt. New York: Seminar Press, 1971, pp. 253-74.

Moon, Eric. "High John." *Library Journal*, 15 Jan. 1968, pp. 147-55.

Moses, Richard. "Hindsight on High John." *Library Journal*, 1 May 1972, pp. 1672-74.

National Book Committee. *Neighborhood Library Centers and Services, a Study by the National Book Committee for the Office of Economic Opportunity*. 2nd ed. New York, 1967.

"Neighborhood Service Centers." In *Encyclopedia of Social Work*. 16th ed. New York: National Association of Social Workers, 1971. 1:857-65.

New York Commissioner of Education's Committee on Library Development. *Report*. Albany: University of the State of New York, 1970.

Niemi, John A. "Conflict or Accommodation? The Need for Articulation Between the Adult Evening School and the Community College." *Continuous Learning*, Jan./Feb. 1970, pp. 31-33.

Nierman, Wayne. "T. Wendell Williams Community Education Center for Coordination of Community Resources." *Community Education Journal*, Feb. 1972, pp. 45-49.

Nyren, Dorothy, ed. *Community Service, Innovations in Outreach at the Brooklyn Public Library.* Chicago: American Library Assn., 1970.

Owens, Major. "A Model Library for Community Action." *Library Journal,* 1 May 1970, pp. 1701-4.

Penland, Patrick. *Floating Librarians in the Community.* Pittsburgh: University of Pittsburgh Press, 1970.

Perlman, Robert, and David Jones. *Neighborhood Service Centers.* Washington, D.C.: Dept. of Health, Education and Welfare, Welfare Administration, Office of Juvenile Delinquency and Youth Development, 1967.

Pettigrew, Thomas F. "The Educational Park Concept." In *Resources for Urban Schools, Better Use and Balance.* Edited by Sterling M. McMurrin. New York: Commission for Economic Development, 1971. (Suppl. paper no. 33), pp. 96-122.

Pings, Vern M. "The Library as a Social Agency, Response to Social Change." *College and Research Libraries,* May 1970, pp. 174-84.

Raines, Max R., and Gunder A. Myran. "Community Services: A University-Community College Approach." *Junior College Journal,* Oct. 1970, pp. 41-42.

Robbins, Jane. "The Reference Librarian: A Street-Level Bureaucrat?" *Library Journal,* 15 Apr. 1972, pp. 1389-92.

Roberts, Don. "Tomorrow's Illiterates." *Library Trends,* Oct. 1971, pp. 297-307.

Shubert, Joseph F., and C. Edwin Dowlin. "Ohio's Books Jobs Program." *Library Journal,* 1 Oct. 1970, pp. 3239-43.

"Slum Storefront Library Serves San Francisco Poor." *Library Journal,* 15 May 1970, p. 1798.

Smith, Eleanor T. "Libraries and Librarians in Our Changing Society." *Minnesota Libraries,* Winter 1969, pp. 339-47.

Smith, Peter J. "Britain's Open University: Everyman's Classroom." *Saturday Review,* 29 Apr. 1972, pp. 40-42, 47-50.

Soule, Gary M. "A Neighborhood Center with a Difference." *Parks and Recreation,* Apr. 1970, pp. 32-34.

Spence, Barbara A. "The Community-Owned Ghetto Library: A Commitment to People." *Bay State Librarian,* Oct. 1969, pp. 11-17.

Spiegel, Hans B. C. "College Relating to Community: Service to Symbiosis." *Junior College Journal,* Aug./Sept. 1970, pp. 30-34.

Sternberg, Eugene, and Barbara Sternberg. *Community Centers and Student Unions.* New York: Van Nostrand, 1971.

Stone, C. Walter. *A Library Program for Columbia.* Pittsburgh: The author, 1965.

Toffler, Alvin. *Future Shock,* New York: Bantam, 1970.

Totten, W. Fred. "Community Education—Best Hope for Society." *School and Society,* Nov. 1970, pp. 410-13.

Towards a Common Goal, School-Public Library Cooperation, Selected Articles. Albany: University of the State of New York, State Education Dept., Division of Library Development, 1968.

U.S. Congress. Senate. Committee on Government Operations. Hearings before the Subcommittee on Executive Reorganization. *Federal Role in Urban Affairs.* 89th Cong., 2nd ses.-90th Cong., 1st ses. Washington, D.C.: Government Printing Office, 1966-67. 20 parts.

Ward, Edward J. *The Social Center.* National Municipal League Series. New York: D. Appleton & Co., 1914.

Warren, Roland L., ed. *Perspectives on the American Community, a Book of Readings.* Chicago: Rand McNally, 1966.

Wedemeyer, Charles A., and M. Habeeb Ghatala. "Wisconsin's Proposed 'Open' School." *Audiovisual Instructor,* Jan. 1972, pp. 9-12.

Welbourne, James. *The Urban Information Specialist Program: First Year; a Report Prepared for the Library Profession.* College Park, Md.: University of Maryland, School of Library and Information Services, 1971.

Zigerell, James J. "Chicago's TV College." *AAUP Bulletin,* Spring 1967, pp. 49-54.

APPENDIX B

Merger without Jeopardy: An Overview of the Olney Project

JAMES A. KITCHENS

Olney, Texas, is an agricultural and oil community of approximately 4,000 people, located in North Central Texas. Confronting all of the problems of a small town in an urban society, Olney faces the threat of economic extinction and a slowly degenerating quality of life. For the past several years the town has waged war for its existence economically by the successful enticement of small industries into the community and by competing for federal assistance through such agencies as Urban Renewal. Concerned citizens are aware that more is involved in staying alive than economic vitality. The town has therefore sought to maintain and develop programs geared to increasing the quality of life among its citizens.

With a better way of life for all citizens in mind, and as a part of a more comprehensive plan, the Olney citizens have sought to improve the intellectual and informational atmosphere of their community. As part of this objective, they conceived a merger of the elementary, junior high, and high school libraries with the city's public library. Such a combination, they felt, held the promise of improved library and information services for all citizens of the community.

These circumstances in Olney represent a unique opportunity to survey, from the very beginning, the process and problems associated with the merging of school and public libraries. Likewise, this library venture offers the possibility of a controlled experiment to evaluate the effectiveness of a merged library, to isolate variables

James A. Kitchens is Assistant Professor, Department of Sociology, North Texas State University, Denton, Texas.

which contribute to the degree of effectiveness achieved, and to study the factors of community organization which impinge upon the utility and feasibility of such a venture for other American small towns.

PURPOSE

The purpose of this project is to assess the success, or nonsuccess, of the attempt of the city of Olney, Texas, to combine the facilities and services of the school libraries and the public library in their city. Specifically, the project is devised to determine the degree of success of their efforts to merge the libraries' functions, the problems associated with the combined libraries, the social and economic variables associated with the results of the combination, and the process of planning and implementation through which the community passes in their library venture. Further, the project is designed to offer consultation to the citizens and various committees concerning planning, staffing, supplying, and servicing the new library.

OBJECTIVES

The following objectives are focal points for the research involved in the project:

1. To discover those social, economic, and political variables associated with the success and nonsuccess of a library and information service program which attempts to defy tradition and combine the functions of the public library and the school libraries in a small city
2. To isolate specific social, political, legal, and library practice problems encountered in the process of combining a public library and school libraries in a small city
3. To discover aspects of library education which may be deficient in preparing administrators and staff for merged public and school libraries
4. To assess the feasibility of a combined public and school library for total library service—including service to early childhood, career development, preparation of school age youngsters for the world of work, and service to adults
5. To discover and describe the process of community organization through which a small city passes in planning and implementing a combined school and public library

6. To improve methodologies of library and community research
7. To seek interagency state and federal funding sources for materials, etc., available to the small community library
8. To develop a model of planning, policies, and implementation of a combined public and school library which may be used in other small towns and rural villages.

DESCRIPTION OF ACTIVITIES

The project is funded for three years, and will be carried out in the following phases. Beginning in January, 1972, work has progressed on two levels. First, there has been an effort to increase community involvement in planning the facilities and its program. Meetings of concerned citizens in workshop type situations led by experts in library services has allowed legitimate community input into the program to be carried out in the merged library. Every effort has been made to increase community awareness of potential library services by showing films, visiting outstanding libraries, and in informal discussions. These meetings have capitalized upon and further generated enthusiasm in the community for the innovative and pathfinding experiment they have ventured upon.

Survey research is being prepared related to the use of present library facilities and their evaluation. A survey of the four library collections is being made to measure their quantity, quality, duplication, and compatibility. Shelf lists are being made of the four book collections so that they may be interfiled to determine the amount of duplication and the extent to which the collections will complement each other. This shelf list will also facilitate the actual merging of the collections in the future. The H. W. Wilson catalogs and other standard bibliographies are being checked to measure the quality of the four book collections.

A community survey is being prepared which will help to answer the following questions: Who uses the public library, why do they use it, and what are the present community attitudes toward the library? What are student attitudes toward the school library? What are the circulation statistics, service statistics, audiovisual statistics for both the public and school libraries? What public information activities are presently being employed? What categories of potential clientele are being omitted from service (old, physically handicapped, poor, ethnic, etc.)? What uses are being made of the Texas State Library's referral facilities by the public library? To what extent are the present facilities of the school libraries supportive of the curriculum, and what demands on the library are made by the faculty? Is career development emphasized? What are the qualifications of the staffs of the present libraries? What are their budgets?

These data will provide baselines from which improvements in services and facilities offered by the new library can be measured in the third year. These data will be collected by means of structured interview schedules administered by professional interviewers. The library staff and school faculty, coupled with other persons responsible for the administration of the library staff and school faculty and other persons responsible for the administration of the library, will serve as respondents. Approximately twenty such persons will be selected by judgmental sample.

Additionally, this survey will compile a description of the community. For a complete analysis of the success or nonsuccess of the new library to be carried out, several variables characteristic of the community at large must be isolated. This step is also necessary for the results of the study to be generalized to other communities. All pertinent socioeconomic and demographic characteristics of the community must be described. (This information will also be useful in uncovering potential service patterns for the new library.) Further, community attitudes toward libraries, schools, and intellectual pursuits in general are seen as significant variables. Community integration and civic pride will have to be analyzed. Observation of planning meetings to discover decision-making processes will be necessary. Analysis of the mass media's coverage of such meetings and the actual construction and equipping of the buildings (as well as the effect upon public attitudes of that coverage) must be made.

During this time the search for interagency state and federal funding agencies will begin. Also the legal structure surrounding libraries will be surveyed for potential problems associated with a merged public and school library. Furthermore, difficulties of a merged library arising from library standards will be analyzed.

Data related to the community will be collected by three methods:

1. Analysis of census records. Descriptive statistics of demographic community data will be drawn from census records.
2. Participant observation of policy planning meetings. Content analysis of taped meetings will be performed on all data gathered in this manner.
3. Personal interview of approximately 150 randomly selected community residents. Using structured interview schedules, data will be gathered on community attitudes, class levels, power structure, and other demographic characteristics to supplement census records. Likert and Guttman

scaling techniques will be used to generate all attitude scales.

The major thrust of the research during the second year will be to determine the effect on the community of publicity and construction of the building and problems associated with preparing for the new library: e.g., orientation of volunteer workers, procurement of materials, movement of materials from old facilities to new, and staffing. Among the specific questions to be answered are: Have there been any significant changes in the use of financial resources for, and attitudes toward, the present facilities? Of interest during this time will also be the mass media's coverage of construction and the effect of that coverage (and other types of dissemination of public information) on public opinion. What library staff changes have taken place during this year, and what is the direction and significance of these changes? Stages in acquiring a staff and furnishing and equipping the library will be delineated and problems associated with these factors uncovered.

Observation of policy planning meetings will be necessary during the second year. Problems associated with the decision making, political and legal restrictions, and policy will be noted. Also, there will be a continuing analysis of census data related to demographic characteristics of the community during the second year.

These data will be collected by means of structured interview schedules and participant observation. Personal interviews will be administered to approximately 200 randomly selected community residents. Content analysis will be done on data collected by participant observation of planning and decision-making meetings. All data will be coded and transferred to computer cards, and proper parametric and nonparametric statistical techniques will be used in data analysis.

During the second year a professional librarian will be employed to work full-time in planning and equipping the new library. This person will be retained by the city as head librarian for the library after actual operation begins.

The third year of the study will be spent primarily in evaluation of the total new library program in the community. Data related to the library similar to that collected in the first year will again be gathered for comparative purposes. Significant socioeconomic changes which may have occurred during the study period will be evaluated for their possible effect upon the success or nonsuccess of the library. Methods introduced to enable the library to support the school curriculum and career development opportunities will be evaluated for their utility and serviceability. Aspects of library services devoted to the service of special interest clientele and to publicizing the overall facilities of the library will be evaluated for their possible positive and/or negative effect. Specific problems growing out of the combination of school libraries and public library will be analyzed as to cause and possible remedy. Methods by which problems are resolved will be reported as well as unsuccessful attempts to ameliorate problems. Difficulties stemming from staffing, book selection, and circulation will be elucidated along with problems related to budgeting and control of facilities.

Three methods of data collection will be used:

1. Participant observation of policy planning meetings. Content analysis will be done on data gathered by this method. All subjective evaluations will be labeled as such in the relevant report.
2. In-depth interviews of approximately fifty influentials and persons responsible for various aspects of the education and library services.
3. Personal interview with approximately 150 randomly selected community residents (including students). Structured interview schedules will be administered by professional interviewers.

CONCLUSION

The questions which this project is designed to answer are significant. During the last several decades, school and public libraries have operated as separate agencies in all sizes of communities, and the library profession has consistently encouraged the distinction through support of library laws, development of library standards, training and education of personnel, and with numerous writings on the *relationship*, as distinguished from the *merger*, of the two types of libraries. A review of the literature reveals that the subject of merging school and public library functions, to be performed in a community center building, has received scant consideration. There have been efforts to combine school and public libraries, generally by locating the public library service in the school building. Ordinarily these projects have not benefited from empirical evaluation of effectiveness. Positive results have, therefore, been difficult to substantiate, and the whole question of the feasibility of merger has been left as a matter of subjective opinion.

With the advent of the concept of *total community library service*, and the emphasis on *access, systems, networks*, and *interlibrary cooperation*—all coming with some force within the past decade—

institutional patterns sanctioned by tradition have been called into question. This project creates the opportunity to study empirically the feasibility of merging the functions of these two types of libraries.

Further, the significance of the problem is associated with the dilemma of the small town in America. Confronted with a shrinking tax base due to population attrition and the demand for expansion of social services, the small town, like large urban centers, must find creative solutions to financial problems. Wise use of tax funds is a necessity. The feasibility of merging the public library and school libraries and thereby increasing efficiency of library service amounts to a potential method of improving the use of the tax dollar and increasing the social services of the community to its citizens. Therefore, the discovery of problems associated with the merging of these problems offers a potentially significant contribution to the fields of library science and community development as well as valuable information for small towns across this country.

In the last analysis, the purpose of the library in any community is to make available in a readily usable form information needed by every segment of the people of the community. Ideally, all service groups of whatever age, ethnicity, educational or vocational background, interest orientation, and class level are to have their intellectual and informational needs met. This program is dedicated to that end. Can public and school libraries be merged in a small town in such a way as to increase overall efficiency in library functions and without jeopardy to any actual or potential library user?

APPENDIX C

The Philadelphia Project: The Action Library, Its Purpose and Program

LOWELL A. MARTIN

The Action Library has one central purpose: to develop ways within the inner city to bridge the gap between young people and learning resources. The new Action Library will seek to accomplish this purpose through:

1. A community-based project, which is free of the traditional restrictions of established schools and libraries
2. A community-oriented program, which involves students and other persons from the neighborhood in most aspects of its operation, including staffing
3. Provision of multimedia resources selected to interest children and young people
4. A multistaff mix, including service teams of librarians, teachers, and other specialists
5. Involvement of parents in the learning process, as well as children and young people
6. Activities designed to attract and stimulate young people and to develop their interests (rather than simply to be available for those with the initiative to seek out the center)
7. Interagency sponsorship by the school systems and the public library, with the overall goal of fostering change in these library systems.

Lowell A. Martin is Consultant to the Philadelphia Project.

RESEARCH BASE

The Action Library is an outgrowth of two years of research into student use of learning media. The Philadelphia Project's research staff studied this use by children and young people in the city's public, parochial, and independent schools, starting with the assignments made by teachers and including the print and audiovisual materials actually used by students, both for school purposes and because of personal interests. These extensive research studies included evaluations of the media which are available to students in both school and public libraries, in relation to student needs.

The results of this research show that while materials sometimes fall short of meeting student needs, the solution to the problem of how to increase student use is not to be found in library collections themselves. The considerable resources which are now available are not being used anywhere near their limit by many young people. Some elements in the educational process or in the experience of growing up increasingly turn a large percentage of students away from learning materials, as these young people (particularly those in the inner city) advance in the formal educational program. Children for whom education has begun as an opening up of the world of recorded knowledge often grow into young people who actually reject the use of learning resources.

If the problem were solely that resources are lacking, the solution would be to build up libraries. The problem, however, is more complex and involves not just the size and level of collections, but also the environment in which they are presented, the motivation aroused for their use, the guidance given in the process, and the elimination of the frustration which the student encounters. The young person goes to the library hoping that the knowledge gathered there will lead him to greater understanding of a subject or perhaps to completion of an assignment. Too often a connection is not made, the gap between the student and the learning materials is not bridged, and the young person comes to feel that somehow he has failed. After several such attempts he decides that libraries, librarians, books, and other media represent false hopes in the educational process.

The Philadelphia research reveals that these deficiencies are found particularly in the inner city, where bridging the gap between the student and learning materials is increasingly crucial. Opportunity to learn is closed, of course, to any young person who does not learn to read. But even for the many who do learn to read the benefits of access to the world of print and other communication forms are denied if they do not use learning materials.

Based on these research findings, the Interagency Committee which is sponsoring the Philadelphia Project decided that there is a need for an experimental demonstration in the form of a library-student learning center. After further study they agreed that the new center should be located in a low-income area in central Philadelphia.

OBJECTIVES

The primary goal of the Action Library is to bridge the gap between young people and learning resources. This overall goal may be divided into three aims:

1. To expose children and young people to new stimuli related to their own identities and the prospects before them as individuals
2. To motivate them to learn more about these prospects, as a means of self-development
3. To guide the inner city student in the continued use of materials of learning so that this use becomes an integral part of his life style.

To meet these aims, the Action Library will endeavor to provide materials and information in all media which serve these purposes.

The Philadelphia Project staff has no illusions that their goals can be achieved for all young people, or that the full sequence (from occasional response to habitual use) will be followed by all those who can be enticed to start. The Action Library, however, will provide an opportunity to try a fresh approach and then to measure the program using such criteria as the number of individuals reached, the range and level of response, the degree to which information is sought, the extent of the use of learning media, and the effect on the use of school and public libraries. Evaluation will be continuous and programs will be added, adjusted, replaced, and expanded as the Action Library's experience and data are measured and analyzed.

PROGRAM

The research data of the Philadelphia Project clearly reveal problems, but the data do not define solutions. At this point neither the project's Interagency Committee nor its staff knows definitively how to bring inner city students into meaningful relation with learning resources. In establishing the Action Library, the Project will attempt to create a setting which will facilitate innovation, and then to draw on its research findings as the staff explores ways to link young people to learning media.

The project's staff, with consultants, have formulated preliminary plans for the Action Library. The entire program will be one of exploration and flexibility, seeking ideas from professionals, parents, and young people themselves, and continuously evaluating results.

It was determined that the program would serve a neighborhood rather than a large community base which often does not exist in the inner city. Plans called for housing the program in a new setting in the neighborhood, not in an already existing school or library. The resources provided were not meant to be primarily those needed to complete school assignments nor those needed for extensive research (the school and public libraries have resources for these purposes), but rather to be those which would stimulate learning, to support the Action Library's activities, provide successful experiences in seeking information, and relate to immediate interests growing out of personal concerns and neighborhood and family life.

In form, resources will probably include as much nonprint as print, and their use will often involve the handling and reaction of the young people. The program will focus on learning *activities* for which resources will be provided, rather than on collections of materials which might be available in another institution. Personalities, happenings, drama, art, crafts, manipulative displays, games, films, and various other means will be used to attract the disenchanted student and to introduce him to recorded knowledge. For example, rather than a black heritage collection of materials, the center might offer a black culture workshop. The whole approach will be to offer something sufficiently appealing to draw young people to the Action Library simply to find out what is going on.

The Action Library will offer activities to individuals working with or without guidance, and to small groups working with a specialist, such as a teacher, librarian, reading specialist, or crafts director. Assistance and training in locating information will be provided for persons who are motivated to search but who lack the skills to use the resources. In the case of young children, parents as well as youngsters will be involved in the learning process. The staff will encompass a variety of professionals with whom the student has previously had contact, such as teachers, librarians, and community workers. At the Action Library, however, these professionals will work complementarily and informally with individuals and groups rather than in formal structured situations. Some of Philadelphia's most effective teachers, librarians, storytellers, and reading guidance experts, many on a part-time basis, will be involved in the Action Library's programs, both in planning and in carrying out. The Action Library will recruit local residents to help as experienced professionals, consultants, and as staff— and will train them as necessary. Older children will help those who are younger in learning activities. A community worker will talk to neighborhood groups, visit homes, and maintain continuous contact between residents and the Action Library.

RELATION TO SCHOOLS AND LIBRARIES

The key to understanding the goals of the Action Library is *not* to think first in organizational terms, such as whether the school library or the public library or some other agency should serve the young student. Philadelphia has such libraries and of relatively good quality, yet still, in the inner city, the gap exists between student and materials. Rather, the way to begin is to think first of children and young people estranged from the materials through which education occurs, and then of activities designed to establish or re-establish contact between the two. The emphasis of the Action Library's programming will not be on the traditional educational concept of instruction, nor on the traditional library concept of building a collection, but on *learning activities* and on *resource media* for those activities.

The approach through a neighborhood agency is consistent with other experimental educational programs. Philadelphia's Parkway Program uses the central institutions of the city as functional classrooms for secondary students. At the elementary level, the city's minischools, which are located away from regular school buildings, seek freedom and motivation for younger children in their own neighborhoods. The common elements in such varying programs are: a fresh start in a noninstitutional setting; activities that facilitate individual development; and informal relationships between the student and a variety of instructional personnel.

Philadelphia residents do not look on these as counter schools. On the contrary, they are designed to provide learning experience that will help students get full benefit from established educational programs. Similarly, the Philadelphia Project's Action Library will not be a counter library, but an attempt to develop library users in a part of the urban environment where there have been all too few of them.

SPONSORING AGENCIES

The Philadelphia Project is funded by the U.S. Office of Education, and is a joint venture by the institutions that have responsibility for education in Philadelphia's inner city: the public schools, the Archdiocesan schools, the private and independent schools, and The Free Library of Philadelphia. The Board of Education serves as the fiscal agent for the federal grants (Higher Education Act and Elementary and Secondary Education Act) that finance the project. The Free Library also administers an LSCA grant for the Action Library. The Interagency Committee which has guided the project from the start and will continue to do so, includes representatives of Philadelphia's two major school systems, and of The Free Library, independent schools, and colleges.

Throughout the research and planning phases of the program, the project has been directed and staffed by the Philadelphia Student Library Research Center. The Center will continue to play an essential role in the evaluation of the program of the Action Library. The project's staff will share information about the Action Library's activities and results with Philadelphia educators and librarians and also will report nationally through the educational and library press.

CURRENT STATUS

By early 1971, the two-year investigation of student use of learning resources had been completed and a limited study of parents' attitudes in relation to student use had been made. An experienced community worker and long-time resident of the area chosen for the Action Library was then added to the staff to increase local involvement in planning.

In November, 1971, a community Advisory Board was established. It is composed of representatives of students, parents, organizations, churches, businesses, and the handicapped from the community. It is serving as a vehicle for the expression and discussion of community aspirations and needs with respect to the Action Library, and it provides liaison between the Action Library and the community. The Board participates in most aspects of the Action Library's operation. The results of the survey that was conducted in late 1971 among families in the community are being used to determine community preferences in various aspects of the Library's operation.

An excellent facility was secured for the Action Library in the community. It occupies space in the St. Charles Borromeo Community Hall, which is located at 20th and Christian Streets, the approximate geographic center of the community. The facility offers nearly 10,000 square feet of space, functionally arranged. It is the center for a number of community activities; therefore, it has the advantage of attracting a number of community residents for a variety of reasons.

Opening date for the Action Library was March 27, 1972, with the official dedication on May 10. The collections, equipment, and furnishings were delivered during the early months of operation and the staff began a variety of programs and activities, to work out for themselves a smooth operating procedure.

Evaluation of the Action Library and its programs has already begun; several evaluators are a part of the Library Project Staff, whose job is to keep complete records of all of the activities related to an evaluation of the Action Library, according to the evaluation design which has been submitted to the Office of Education. An education audit of the Library Project is being conducted independently by an auditor. As reports and results of the Action Library activities and programs are obtained, the project staff will attempt to disseminate them widely for purposes of transferability to other libraries and educational institutions throughout the country.

ALA-NEA
Joint Committee
and Other
Conference
Participants

COMMITTEE MEMBERS

Dorothy Dagon (NEA), Elementary Classroom Teacher, Barber School, Phillipsburg, New Jersey

Glenn R. Dallman (ALA), Director of Library Services, Clearwater Campus, St. Petersburg Jr. College, Clearwater, Florida

Sidney Dorros (NEA Staff Liaison), Communications Program Consultant, NEA Communications Division, Washington, D.C.

C. Edwin Dowlin (ALA), State Librarian, New Mexico State Library, Santa Fe, New Mexico

*Harriett A. Drilling (NEA), Media Specialist, Miramar High School, Hollywood, Florida

*Guy Garrison (ALA), Dean, Graduate School of Library Science, Drexel University, Philadelphia, Pennsylvania

*Philip A. Gonyar (NEA), Social Studies Department Head, Bangor Public Schools, Bangor, Maine

Jay Hunter (NEA), Elementary Classroom Teacher, Wichita Public Schools, Wichita, Kansas

*James Igoe (ALA), State Librarian, Vermont State Library, Montpelier, Vermont

Alice Perlaw (NEA), Librarian, Madison High School, Madison, New Jersey

*Grace Slocum (ALA), Assistant Director, Enoch Pratt Free Library, Baltimore, Maryland

Positions are listed as of May, 1972.

*Indicates Conference Planning Subcommittee

Ruth Warncke (ALA Staff Liaison), Deputy Executive Director, American Library Association, Chicago, Illinois

PARTICIPANTS

Augusta Baker, Coordinator of Children's Services, New York Public Library, New York, New York.

Alvia Barfield, President-Elect, Association of Classroom Teachers, National Education Association, Washington, D.C.

Catherine Barrett, President-Elect, National Education Association (represented by Dorothy Dagon as member of NEA Board of Directors)

Toni Carbo Bearman, Student, Drexel University, Philadelphia, Pennsylvania

Kenneth Beasley, Dean of the Graduate School, University of Texas—El Paso, El Paso, Texas

Gerald R. Brong, Assistant Director, Audiovisual Center, Washington State University, Pullman, Washington

Kenneth Carruthers, Vice President, Doxiadis Associates, Inc., Washington, D.C.

Charles Churchwell, Director of Libraries, Miami University, Oxford, Ohio

Edmond R. Coletta, Supervising Budget Analyst, State House, Providence, Rhode Island

Ralph W. Conant, Director, Southwest Center for Urban Research, Houston, Texas

Keith Doms, President, American Library Association and Director, Free Library of Philadelphia, Philadelphia, Pennsylvania

Arthur Dorros, Student, University of Wisconsin, Madison Wisconsin

Ruth Frame, Executive Secretary, Library Administration Division, American Library Association, Chicago, Illinois

Mildred Frary, Director, Library Services, Los Angeles City Unified School District, Los Angeles, California

John B. Geissinger, Superintendent of Schools, Tenafly, New Jersey

Jewell Harris, Director of Information Services, Abilene Public Schools, Abilene, Texas

Frances Hatfield, Coordinator of Instructional Materials, School Board of Broward County, Ft. Lauderdale, Florida

Robert Heinich, Professor of Education, Audiovisual Center, Indiana University, Bloomington, Indiana

Anna Hyer, Division of Instruction and Professional Development, National Education Association, Washington, D.C.

F. J. Johnson, Professional Services Coordinator, Association of Classroom Teachers, Washington, D.C.

S. Janice Kee, Library Services Program Officer, Regional Office, U.S. Office of Education, Dallas, Texas

James A. Kitchens, Assistant Professor, Department of Sociology, North Texas State University, Denton, Texas

Rita Kososky, Teacher, Walt Whitman High School, Bethesda, Maryland

Allie Beth Martin, Director, Tulsa City-County Library System, Tulsa, Oklahoma

Maria Martinez, Elementary Classroom Teacher, Albuquerque Public Schools, Albuquerque, New Mexico

Kathleen Molz, Chief of Planning, Bureau of Libraries and Learning Resources, U.S. Office of Education, Department of Health, Education and Welfare, Washington, D.C.

Robert Myers, Associate Dean, School of Business Administration, Miami University, Oxford, Ohio

A. Harry Passow, Jacob A. Schiff Professor of Education, Teachers College, Columbia University, New York, New York

Roderick Swartz, Deputy Secretary, National Commission on Libraries and Information Science, Washington, D.C.

Charles Tate, Special Assistant to the President, The Urban Institute, Washington, D.C.

Nettie B. Taylor, Assistant State Superintendent for Libraries, Maryland State Department of Education, Baltimore, Maryland

J. Lloyd Trump, Associate Secretary for Research and Development, National Association of Secondary School Principals, Washington, D.C.

Lu Ouida Vinson, Executive Secretary, American Association of School Librarians, Chicago, Illinois

FLARE